A Photographic History
Colorado

Snowmass, 2009. Author

John English

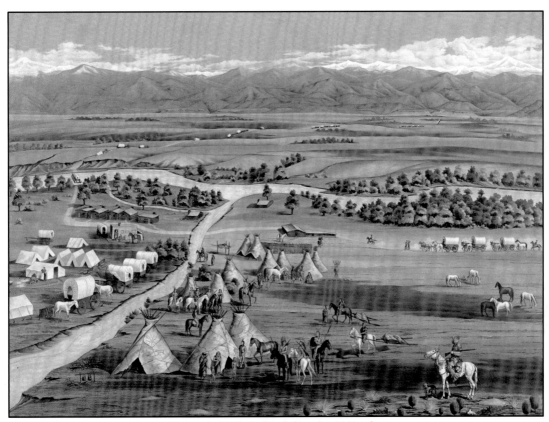

Denver in 1859. Collier & Cleveland Litho Co.

A Photographic History of
Colorado

At left, the crew on the deck of the U.S.S. Colorado, c.1863 (A gift to the Library of Congress by Col. Godwin Ordway in 1948.)

ISBN-10:0-9635669-1-1
ISBN-13:978-0-9635669-1-1
Pronghorn Publishing, an imprint of BHSW Inc.
Old City Hall Building
606 6th. Avenue
Belle Fourche SD 57717

Other Books by John English

Fiction: Murder on the Missouri (novel, Pronghorn Publishing)

                Waves (short stories, Pronghorn Publishing)

How To: The Gout Book (Pronghorn Publishing)

                The Building Buddy (Pronghorn Publishing)

                The Woodworker's Guide to Sharpening (Fox Chapel Publishing)

                Bench Planes & Scrapers (Linden Publishing)

                Turning Wood with Carbide Tools (Linden Publishing)

                Harvest Your Own Lumber (Linden Publishing)

History: The Black Hills, A History in Photographs (Pronghorn Publishing)

                The Cowboy Story, A History in Photographs (Pronghorn Publishing)

All titles are available at bhsw.org

Dedication

To my grandchildren,
who are all dreams come true.

Acknowledgements:

My thanks on behalf of all Americans to the wonderful folks at the
Library of Congress, *who help preserve our nation's identity.*
They were the primary source for these images.
Donations to the Library are tax deductible.
To donate, visit loc.gov/philanthropy

And my deepest gratitude goes to the intrepid photographers,
without whom we would only have words.

Contents

At left is a view of what is recorded as the first large church built in Denver (it was Methodist). The structure was located at what is now the east corner of Lawrence and 14th. This image was made c.1867, probably by William Gunnison Chamberlain. Construction began in 1865 and the sanctuary was dedicated in 1867. By 1910 the architecture had become simplified with the removal of several of the small spires, and the building had become a barracks of the Salvation Army. The land once occupied by the church is now part of the site of another building topped by a spire that reaches for the heavens, the magnificent new Four Seasons Hotel.

Introduction

The most familiar aspect of Colorado is its topography. Those massive peaks, raging rivers and permanent snowcaps have always been a challenge to animals, plants and people, but they have also been a huge attraction. Today, Colorado hosts almost sixty million visitors each year, and while many travel here in summer to enjoy Alpine meadows and mountaintop drives, others come in shorter days for winter sports.

Moving through the mountains wasn't always as easy as it is today. The geomorphology of the state is as diverse as anywhere on the planet, and that is the key to human settlement in Colorado. Because of ice on the Rockies, it was only very recently (some sixteen thousand years ago) that people finally began to transcend that barrier as a matter of course.

While it touches on those ancient roots, the bulk of this book concentrates on the years since the Civil War, because that's when photography became commercially viable. European settlement of Colorado began in earnest around the same time, so there is a rich visual archive of the period. Choosing which images to include was not easy, but the folks at the Library of Congress were especially helpful as a source of photographs. They deserve our eternal gratitude for preserving our national identity.

Settling on the story itself was a task, too. The title of this book suggests that this is *a* history, and not *the* definitive history of the state. Leaving out a small detail or a simple nuance can completely change the way a record reads, or perhaps the shape of a personality. Keep in mind that most of the content here has been subject to many decades of revision. It is imperative that all sides are presented, and indeed that is not the challenge. What is most difficult is deciding in what measure each facet appears, so that the whole is not unbalanced. And there lies the crux: one hundred and sixty centuries of Native settlement and, in relative terms, just a very brief period of European influence.

Written history is, by its very nature, subjective.

The dates attributed herein to photographs are, by and large, accurate. However, the actual vintage of a few images has been estimated, when complete records were not available. And while every effort was made to identify the photographers there are still a few unattributed images, and those are noted in the captions.

Speaking of dates, AD has now become CE (Common Era), and BC is BCE (Before Common Era). One assumes the change was motivated by political correctness, but the actual dynamics are elusive: the new format is still based on the estimated birth date of Jesus of Nazareth.

Oh, well…

Chapter 1
Ancient Roots

At the end of the Pleistocene era, the earth experienced what is popularly known as the last Ice Age. This occurred about 110,000 to 12,000 years ago, depending on location. It was the final freeze in what had been some two million years of glacial activity. As the ice receded, people began crossing the Bering land bridge from Asia. These Paleo-Americans (Paleo comes from the Greek word for 'old') had a simple hunting/gathering culture and they followed grass-eating herds of animals into Alaska. As the ice sheet retreated, some of the more adventurous worked their way down the Rockies. By about 11,000 years ago, a few began to settle in the foothills below the eastern slopes.

In 1924, three archeological enthusiasts discovered relics of an ancient settlement on the land of William Lindenmeier, a rancher in what is now Larimer County, Colorado (halfway across the northern edge of the state, on the border with Wyoming). Subsequent explorations have revealed that these ancient people were members of the Folsom tradition. That is, they had adapted their hunting methods to smaller game that had replaced woolly mammoths and mastodons, although they still hunted the seven-foot tall precursor to what we now commonly call buffalo, *Bison Antiquus* (at right). These larger animals had begun to disappear, perhaps due to climate change, a meteorological event, disease or even human predation, depending on which theory one espouses.

Graphic showing the approximate relative size of today's American Bison (left) and Bison Antiquus (right).

The men who discovered the find (which was declared a National Historic Landmark in 1961) were Judge Claude Coffin and his son Lynn, and a Forest Ranger who is thought to have been C.K. Collins. Tools, especially spearheads, found at the site were confirmed in 1926 as Folsom artifacts by Dr. E.B. Renaud of the Anthropology Department on the campus of Denver University. During the 1930s and '40s, a team from the Smithsonian Institute worked the site under the direction of Frank Roberts (1897-1966). Roberts was associated with the Bureau of American Ethnology at the Smithsonian.

Through this dig and a similar one in New Mexico, he was ultimately responsible for establishing that there had been people on the North American continent at the same time as the extinct mammals mentioned earlier. In 1960, two radiocarbon dating experts, C. Vance Haynes, Jr. and George Agogino, began work to establish precise dates for the settlement. Thirty-two years later, Haynes and his team published the final results: people had lived in Larimer County between 8650 and 8770 BCE – that is, about 10,700 years ago. These are currently believed to have been the earliest inhabitants of what is now the State of Colorado.

The white cliffs in the photo above probably served as a beacon to ancient Folsom people. The Soapstone Prairie Natural Area shown here includes the Lindenmeier archaeological site, which was excavated by the Smithsonian in the 1930s. Findings from the site have revealed that people lived in modern Colorado far earlier than previously thought – between 10,000 and 12,000 years ago. Today, one can stand in the exact spot where they did and enjoy the splendid silence of a 34-square mile natural area, or hike more than 40 miles of trails through their neighborhood.

Photo by Charlie Johnson, used with permission from Zoë Whyman, City of Fort Collins Natural Areas Department (fcgov.com/naturalareas). At right is an unattributed image of a Folsom point.

Mesa Verde

After the Lindenmeier dig, the next strong evidence of human settlement in Colorado is relatively recent. It occurred less than 1,500 years ago, somewhere around 550 CE. At that time, Pueblo Natives began to establish a settlement on Mesa Verde in the southwest corner of the state (about 370 miles from Denver). On June 29, 1906, President Theodore Roosevelt established Mesa Verde National Park, and here's how the National Park Service describes the site:

"Mesa Verde, Spanish for green table, offers a spectacular look into the lives of the Ancestral Pueblo people who made it their home for over 700 years, from A.D. 600 to 1300. Today the park protects nearly 5,000 known archeological sites, including 600 cliff dwellings. These sites are some of the most notable and best preserved in the United States."

Toward the end of that period, somewhere around 1100 CE, these ancient Puebloans began carving houses into the soft sandstone (the cliff dwellings referred to above). Unfortunately, a drought in the last quarter of the thirteenth century (c.1275-1300 CE) meant that life became unsustainable on the Mesa and many of the Pueblo people moved southeast into the Rio Grande valley. Had they known it, there was ample water just 100 miles northeast of the Mesa, where a mudslide had created a new lake (now known as Lake San Cristobal) about a century earlier.

Today, Mesa Verde National Park is a UNESCO World Heritage Site. Located in Montezuma County, the entrance is just a few minutes east of Cortez on Hwy 160. That's about an hour's drive northeast of where Colorado, Utah, Arizona and New Mexico meet. Today, there are Jicarilla (Apache), Ute, Navajo and Hopi reservations within 200 miles of Mesa Verde. Jicarilla Apache migrated to Colorado and northern New Mexico from Alaska and Canada around 1300 to 1525 CE.

At left is a 2007 photo by Lisa Lynch from the Historic American Building Survey (HABS) Documentation of the Serpents Quarters Pueblo near Cortez. Noted as "Room B, looking north", this image illustrates a number of key facets of the Pueblo building methods, not least of which is the fact that they built with passive solar in mind (the cliff faces south). According to HABS, the Serpents Quarters Pueblo was constructed and occupied during the 12th and 13th centuries, which means these ruins are still standing more than 800 years after they were created.

The HABS report says: "The impressive architecture includes habitation and storage rooms, kivas, and towers. (It includes) an 8-10 room structure and kiva built against an overhanging cliff face with substantial portions of intact painted interior wall plaster and a tower and adjacent room built on an isolated spire 100 meters southeast. Some masonry wall fabric has collapsed, although several structures contain wall segments which stand over 3.9 meters in height."

*The photo **above**, also taken by Lisa Lynch, shows the southwest elevation of a talus structure and the north pueblo structure at Cannonball Pueblo near Cortez.*

In architecture, a talus is a slope that was formed by an accumulation of rock debris. They often occur at the base of tall, unstable cliffs where natural forces have caused erosion. While much of the structure exhibits stack bonding (the rocks line up vertically, one on top of the next), there are also courses where a running bond ties the walls together. For example, the joints in the third and sixth rows from the bottom are staggered.

The same mix of methods can be seen in the view **above** (again, this is Serpents Quarters Pueblo photographed by Lisa lynch). Note the way the cliff base is undercut, and how the structure took full advantage of everything that nature offered. The right side of the picture hints at the view down into the valley and the degree of protection offered by this well-chosen site.

In the previous photograph one could see that, between the two outside faces of the walls which are made up of larger rocks, the cavity between has been filled with fine rubble, small rocks and gravel. These thick walls have enough mass to store energy: the building interiors would be significantly cooler during the day and warmer at night that the ambient air.

Above, a HABS photograph taken sometime after 1933 (the photographer and date are not recorded) shows the Cliff Palace at Colorado's Mesa Verde National Park. Initial construction here dates to about 1400 CE. That same year in the 'civilized' world, a Mongol Horde under Tameralne was invading Syria, Georgia, Russia, and utterly destroying Damascus and Baghdad.

The photograph **below** was taken by Russell Lee as part of an effort by the federal government to record American life in the wake of the Dust Bowl and the Depression. Taken under the auspices of the U.S. Farm Security Administration, it shows tourists visiting the cliff dwellings in Colorado in August 1939, just days before Hitler invaded Poland.

~

Chapter 2
Early Europeans

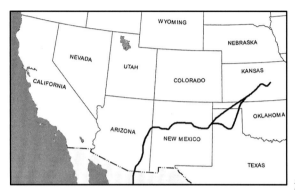

The route of Coronado's expedition in 1541, which initiated Spanish settlement of the area.

Francisco Vázquez de Coronado was born in Salamanca, Spain around 1510, of minor nobility. He made his way to Mexico around his 25th birthday. Through marriage and political contacts, he became the governor of Nueva Galicia, which today is essentially Jalisco and Nayarit, from Guadalajara west to the coast. Six years later in 1541, armed as a Conquistador, he led a military expedition north (depicted in the Frederic Remington painting **below**, which was completed in 1897). His route, shown at left, led from Mexico into what is now Arizona, New Mexico, corners of Texas and Oklahoma, and eventually Kansas. Coronado was following rumors of unimagined wealth (cities of gold) among the Native tribes. To that end, he sent out men in several directions and one of these, Garcia López de Cárdenas, was the first European to see the Grand Canyon.

Although he didn't quite make it to Colorado, Coronado's expedition is important to the story of the state because he introduced European explorers to the area. In his wake, missionaries and soldiers spread across the territory and established contact (not always beneficial) with Native settlements. By 1598, there was a Spanish colony at San Juan de los Caballeros, beside the Ohkay Owingeh Pueblo, which is approximately 100 miles south of Alamosa, Colorado in modern New Mexico. Here, in 1680, the Pueblo people rose up in revolt against their Spanish masters under the leadership of a shaman named Popé.

16

The revolt fanned out from Ohkay Owingeh, eventually driving the Spanish all the way down the Rio Grande to El Paso. The rebellion lasted two years until Diego de Vargas Zapata y Luján Ponce de León y Contreras (Don Diego de Vargas) finally ended resistance.

La Salle

Taking advantage of the situation, the entire northeastern half of modern Colorado was claimed by France that year (1692), and renamed as part of La Louisiane (Louisiana) in honor of King Louis XIV. The claim was established by René-Robert Cavelier, Sieur de La Salle (**at left**, in an engraving possibly by a Dutch artist named Van der Guchi). La Salle was a French explorer who also traveled through the Great Lakes region, down the Mississippi River and along the Gulf of Mexico.

The rest of modern Colorado remained in Spanish/Mexican hands for another century and a half. And the first regional contact between these two empires (France and Spain) didn't happen for another forty-seven years. In the summer of 1739, two French-Canadian brothers, Pierre Antoine Mallet and Paul Mallet, visited the settlement at Santa Fe after becoming the first Europeans to cross the Great Plains. Along the way they rowed up the Missouri to modern South Dakota, and then crossed to the Platte River in Wyoming. This they followed to the South Platte, which they ascended to the Nebraska border in the extreme northeast corner of Colorado (around Julesburg). From there they headed south, probably following the route of modern Highway 385 which runs down the eastern edge of Colorado parallel to the Nebraska and Kansas lines, until they reached the Arkansas River. Following that waterway west and thus deeper into Colorado, they met a party of Comanche near La Junta (about ninety minutes drive southeast of Colorado Springs), who had an Arikara slave. The brothers hired this man to guide them to Santa Fe. He subsequently led them southwest toward modern Trinidad, and then out of Colorado along what would later become the Santa Fe Trail.

One hundred years after LaSalle's bold move, King Louis XV of France (**at right**, in a portrait by Maurice Quentin de La Tour) signed a secret treaty with Spain that once again transferred eastern Colorado and the rest of Louisiana back to Spanish rule. This was the Treaty of Fontainebleau and it was signed after the French and Indian War, which gave Britain control of Canada. It was a ploy to ally the Catholic empires of Spain and France during the latter's

Louis XV

negotiations at the Treaty of Paris (1763), which ended the Seven Years War in Europe. The Paris agreement split Louisiana along the Mississippi, giving Britain everything east of the river, and France everything west.

Count O'Reilly

The next year, King Louis made the secret treaty public. However, a number of French settlers had already moved from the British to the French zone, and they were not pleased to find out that they were now Spanish subjects. They chased the first Spanish governor out of the territory in a rebellion in 1768. They weren't so lucky with the next emissary. Alexander O'Reilly was born in Dublin, Ireland, although his family roots were in Baltrasna, County Meath. He was Catholic, and his grandfather had served with King James II when that sovereign lost his British Crown to the Dutch Protestant, William of Orange.

As a Catholic, O'Reilly (**at left** in a portrait c.1769 by Francisco José de Goya) had no future in Ireland, so he joined the Spanish army where he served in Italy, and then during the invasion of Portugal in 1762. He was promoted to Brigadier General at the age of 40, became a Spanish citizen and changed his first name to Alejandro. He was then posted to Cuba and in 1765 was sent to Puerto Rico to assess and improve that colony's defenses, which he did. While he was doing so the regional governor of Santa Fe, Tomás Vélez Cachupin, sent an expedition into Colorado's San Juan Mountains to chart and explore the region.

On a visit to Spain in 1769 with his new Cuban bride (Doña Rosa de Las Casas, sister of Cuba's Governor), O'Reilly was appointed as the Governor of Louisiana and immediately dispatched with a force of 3,000 to quell the anti-Spanish rebellion by the French. He executed the leaders in New Orleans and began a very brief period of stern but somewhat progressive rule during which he enacted several pieces of anti-slavery legislation. At the end of the year (1769) he resigned his governorship and returned to Spain a hero. The king awarded him by elevating him to the aristocratic rank of Count (the equivalent of an Earl in his native Ireland). He died in Cadiz twenty-five years later of natural causes.

Six years after Count Alejandro O'Reilly returned to Spain, guns were once more heard in North America. In 1775 the American Revolution once again embroiled the great powers in armed conflict. French, Dutch and Spanish support of the Americans turned a regional conflict into an international struggle that eventually involved German mercenaries and even the support of a resistance government in India that was opposing advances by the British East India Company. The militant state of Mysore, governed by Muslim king Nawab Hyder Ali and his son Tipu Sultan, was among the first countries to diplomatically recognize the new United States. They fought a concurrent war against Britain, drawing that country's resources from the conflict in America.

During this turbulent period, Colorado was essentially at peace. In 1776, Franciscan priests searching for a route from Santa Fe to California charted the Colorado Plateau. This is a large and relatively flat high plain that covers the Four Corners area and includes much of eastern Utah, northern Arizona, northwest New Mexico and western Colorado.

The expedition, led by Father Francisco Atanasio Domínguez and Father Silvestre Vélez de Escalante, first entered modern Colorado south of Durango, to the east of Mesa Verde. About forty miles east of Four Corners, they became the first Europeans to record seeing ancient ruins: today, at the Anasazi Heritage Center in Dolores there are two pueblos named after them (Escalante and Domínguez). They then moved north past the San Juan Mountains, roughly paralleling the modern border with Utah, and finally began working eastward when they came in contact with a large group of Ute riders. They spent some time at the Ute village near modern Bowie and then headed north again, crossing the Colorado at Una (about halfway between Grand Junction and Glenwood Springs). From there, they made their way through Rio Blanco County and on into Utah, and from there through Arizona and back east to Santa Fe.

If you're in the San Juan National Forest traveling on Highway 160 about seven miles west of Hesperus in La Plata County, look to your left. A bronze marker (shown **above**) is set in a large sedimentary boulder to mark the date when the two priests and their eight companions passed this spot – August 10, 1776. Coincidentally, that was the same day that King George III learned of the existence of the Declaration of Independence.

The next big event in Colorado history was another secret treaty signed by Spain and France in October of 1800. This one was completed at the palace of La Granja de San Ildefonso in the hills near Segovia, about fifty miles north of Madrid. Under its terms, Spain returned the American territory of Louisiana, which included half of Colorado, at the insistence of Napoleon Bonaparte (1769–1821). In return, Charles IV of Spain received parts of the ancient kingdom of Etruria, which makes up much of modern Tuscany (hugging the west coast of Italy, going north from Rome). This was in turn given to Charles's son-in-law Ferdinand, the Duke of Parma, who had married his daughter Maria Amalia, the Archduchess of Austria. At the time, Napoleon I was Emperor of the French and King of Italy.

It must have rankled these crowned heads to deal with a common man such as Thomas Jefferson, but deal they did. Just three years after the pact made at San Ildefonso, and without Spain's agreement, Napoleon and Jefferson concluded the Louisiana Purchase. Eastern Colorado was, for the first time, part of the United States.

Zebulon Pike was born in what is now Trenton, New Jersey in 1779. In 1805, as an Army lieutenant, he led an expedition to discover the source of the Mississippi at the behest of General James Wilkinson. He and a party of twenty men made it to what is now downtown Minneapolis before winter caught them. Pike and a handful of men then trekked across central Minnesota to Leech Lake, which they decided was the river's source. (The Mississippi actually rises a bit farther north, at Lake Itasca.)

Zebulon Pike

There is some speculation that Pike (**at left**, in an 1808 Charles W. Peale engraving) was actually being used to taunt the British to see how they would react to Americans testing their frontiers. Pike made it home safely, and the next spring (1806) he was sent on another strange mission – this time to test the Spanish reaction to an exploration of the southwest. His first big obstacle was an attempt to scale what is now known as Pike's Peak (which he failed to complete). Then a contingent of Spanish soldiers found Pike and his party on the Conejos fork of the Rio Grande (about 15 miles southeast of Alamosa, Colorado), holed up in a makeshift bastion built with cottonwood logs.

He was escorted first to Santa Fe, and then to Chihuahua, Mexico. Pike then spent a year as a 'guest' of the Spanish. He had been discovered just over the line that divided Colorado – the southwest half was Spanish and the northeast half was American.

One interesting outcome from his travels was the revelation that the general who sent him, James Wilkinson, was actually a double agent, a spy working for the Spanish.

After his Colorado adventure, Pike served in the War of 1812 during which time he became a brigadier general. He led the successful attack on York (Toronto), but unfortunately died there shortly after the battle from a wound.

Above, Pike's Peak is seen from Altman in Teller County, Colorado, almost a century after Pike's attempt to scale the mountain. The settlement burned to the ground three years after this photograph was made. It's now a ghost town. *(Photo by William Henry Jackson, 1900)*

No European scaled Pike's Peak successfully until 1820, when Edwin James accomplished the feat. Half a state south of there, the Spanish still had some misgivings about the French sale of Louisiana, so it was no surprise when, in 1819, they built the only permanent Spanish outpost in Colorado. At the top of the Sangre de Cristo Pass, at an elevation of about 9,500 feet, some one hundred soldiers sat in the snow and waited for the United States to invade Santa Fe. Just two years later, the Spanish-American border was moved when the Adams-Onis Treaty (which also brought Florida into the US) was ratified by Spain, and the fort was abandoned. That same year (1821), Spain recognized Mexico's independence, but it took Mexico until 1831 to ratify the Treaty.

Trade routes to southern Colorado received a boost that fall when William Becknell (aka Bucknell, Bicknell) opened the Santa Fe Trail. Born in Virginia, Becknell was recorded as living in Missouri in 1812, when he served as a ranger. He was involved in the salt trade for a while, and doesn't seem to have been a very good businessman: he was heavily in debt by 1821, when he conceived a plan to hunt wild horses in the southern Rockies. Just over the Raton Pass on the Colorado-New Mexico border, he and his party learned of the Adams-Onis Treaty, and that Santa Fe was now open to American traders. Becknell rushed to town, becoming the first American to do so. He made enough profit to return to Missouri and pay all his debts.

In 1833 three fur traders, William Bent, his brother Charles, and their partner Ceran de Hault de Lassus de St. Vrain, erected a fortified post near what is now La Junta, the county seat of Otero County. The site was on the Arkansas River east of Pueblo, and its purpose was to trade for buffalo hides with the Arapaho and Southern Cheyenne. After a mysterious fire in 1849, the fort was relocated thirty miles or so to the east, near Prowers (named for pioneer John W. Prowers). The drawing **at right** was made by Daniel Jenks in 1859, and includes some groves of planted trees above
the river at the extreme right. Today, the original site of Bent's Fort is home to a reconstructed National Historic Site. (For more information, visit nps.gov.)

22

William Bent was born in St. Louis in 1809, one of eleven children and the son of a Missouri Supreme Court justice. His older brother Charles was the first territorial governor of New Mexico, and a partner in the fur trading business along with two other siblings, George and Robert.

Two years after the first Bent Fort was completed, another trading outlet was built just northeast of the future site of Denver, in 1835. That was the same year Texas revolted against Mexican rule, and established a republic the following spring. The new country nominally included a small portion of modern southeast Colorado. Fort Vasquez stood on the banks of the South Platte River in modern Platteville, and was constructed by two fur trappers, Louis Vasquez and Andrew Sublette. It was sold in 1840 and abandoned in 1842.

In 1836 another fortified trading post was established further along the South Platte, this time by a West Point graduate, Lancaster Platt Lupton. He was a professional soldier who knew little of the fur trade, but Fort Lancaster operated until the blizzard of 1844, after which Lupton moved to California. In 1837, Peter Sarpy and Henry Fraeb established Fort Jackson (it lasted a year), and Bent's old partner Ceran de Hault de Lassus de St. Vrain built Fort Saint Vrain. Both were constructed on the South Platte.

'Civilization' Arrives

Anybody traveling in Wyoming or Colorado will eventually come across the name of John Charles Frémont. While he eventually rose to become an abolitionist candidate for president in 1864 (opposing Lincoln), in the summer of 1842 he was to be found on a steamboat in St. Louis trying to talk Kit Carson into a job. Aged 29, Frémont (**at right**) was a lieutenant in the Corps of Topographical Engineers charged with exploring the route to and through South Pass in Wyoming. For five months the 25-man party moved through the high plains and mountains, following the Kansas and Platte rivers. They brought back maps of the region made by Charles Preuss that included the area south of modern Wyoming to a little north of Colorado Springs, and Frémont became a national celebrity.

John Charles Frémont in an 1861 portrait by L Prang & Co., Boston

23

In the summer of 1846, Brigadier General Stephen Kearney used Colorado as a staging area for a U.S. invasion of Santa Fe, which he successfully completed that August. His initial headquarters were at Bent's Fort. Two years later, Mexico and the United States signed a peace treaty at Guadalupe Hidalgo in Mexico City to end the Mexican American War.

All of Colorado was now, for the first time, in the possession of the U.S.

The following year (1847), John Frémont was court marshaled for mutiny when he refused to give up the military governorship of California, which President Polk had awarded to General Kearney. The disgraced Frémont and his father-in-law, Senator Thomas Hart Benton from Missouri, organized a private expedition to explore the route of a railroad from St. Louis to San Francisco, essentially following the 38th parallel. In November 1848 at Bent's Fort, the trappers there pleaded with Frémont not to proceed into the mountains due to poor weather conditions. Ignoring them, he led ten of his party to their deaths. The remainder of the expedition finally turned around on December 22nd, and arrived in Taos on February 12th.

Frémont left for California, struck gold and became extremely wealthy in 1849. In 1850, he was elected one of the first two senators from the newly created state of California. That same year, a prospector named Lewis Ralston panned the first gold found in Colorado by a European. There were reports made by Cherokee travelers the previous year that they had found placer gold along the Platte. Ralston figured there wasn't enough to make it worth pursuing so he, too, packed his bags and joined the Forty-Niners in California.

Senator Thomas Hart Benton of Missouri, father-in-law to John Frémont, helped finance the disastrous Colorado expedition of 1848.
(Matthew Brady, c.1847)

Chapter 3
The Journey Toward Statehood

In 1850, a sizeable part of southwestern Colorado became part of the new Territories of Utah and New Mexico. Four years later, Kansas and Nebraska Territories enveloped the eastern part of modern Colorado. The New Mexico Territory included the site of San Luis de la Culebra, the oldest town in modern Colorado, 18 miles north of the border. (It was actually in New Mexico until 1861, when the territory of Colorado was established.) The village was built around the church of Saint Louis, a thirteenth century French bishop who died at the age of 23. He was a champion of the poor, and indeed San Luis de la Culebra is still in need of his patronage: as of the 2000 Census, one third of the town's population was still living below the federal poverty line. However, it is also home to a vibrant effort to retain its history. On its website (museumtrail.org/SanLuisMuseum.asp), the San Luis Museum and Cultural Center says that "here you will find the 'vega', one of the two remaining 'commons' in the United States, the oldest water rights in Colorado, and the oldest family store in the state".

The San Luis valley was also the site of the first United States military base in Colorado, Fort Massachusetts. Established in 1852 by Major George Blake, it was home to the First Dragoons and their mission was to protect trade routes from hostile Utes and Jicarilla Apaches. It was replaced by Fort Garland, six miles closer to Santa Fe, in 1858.

Antoine Janis, far right in the back row, was the first recorded settler in northern Colorado. To his right are Joe Merrivale and Young Spotted Tail (Lakota). In the front row are Touch-the-Clouds; Little Big Man; Black Cool and an unidentified person. The image, c.1875, is possibly by Matthew Brady.

That was the same year –1858 – that the town of LaPorte was formally founded by the fur trader Antoine Janis (previous page). He was the first recorded permanent white settler in northern Colorado. Janis, a native of Missouri, spent much of his childhood traveling in the company of his father who traded along the Colorado/Wyoming border country. He married into a Lakota (Sioux) tribe and settled on the Cache la Poudre River in Larimer County in 1844. The town is just six miles northwest of Fort Collins, and was actually the site of traders' cabins all the way back to 1828. Kit Carson wintered there in 1849. Originally, the charter for the town named it Colona, but it was changed to LaPorte in 1862 when it became a stagecoach stop on the Overland Trail.

One of the oldest photographs of Colorado (**above**) was taken by Solomon Nunes Carvalho. He was born in Charleston, South Carolina in 1815. His father was one of the founders of the reformed Society of Israelites, and the son was a respected Jewish community leader.

Carvalho earned renown as a portrait painter (his work even appeared on some U.S. currency notes), and after the invention of the daguerreotype, as a photographer. In 1848, he was part of Frémont's disastrous search for a railroad route through Kansas, Colorado and Utah. He escaped with his life, but not his photographic plates. Only this one survived…

It is purported to show a Cheyenne village at Big Timbers on the Arkansas, just west of the present day Kansas state line. While only two seem visible, there apparently were four large tipis standing at the edge of a wooded area. There is a frame with pemmican or hides hanging at the right, and two figures, facing the camera, standing to the left. The Library of Congress has listed the publication date as 1853. It was probably made in 1848 or possibly even 1849, and took a while to be published. A man of many hats, Carvalho later patented a steam engine, and also founded the first Jewish organization in Los Angeles, the Hebrew Benevolent Society.

The Founding of Denver

On a warm afternoon in the first week of July 1858, in the shallows of Little Dry Creek in eastern Colorado, William Greeneberry Russell struck gold. He and his partner Sam Bates found a small deposit of placer gold – about twenty ounces. This was the beginning of the Pike's Peak Gold Rush. A settlement quickly formed in Russell Gulch, which today is a virtual ghost town. It was located two miles southwest of Central City, about forty miles due west of downtown Denver, at an altitude of 9150 feet. At its peak in 1900, the town was home to 728 souls. That November (1858), Russell started a new town just south of the confluence of Cherry Creek and the South Platte River, which he called Auraria. (Today, it is a neighborhood within the city of Denver). Three weeks later William Larimer, a Kansas State legislator and real estate developer, platted a new city across the creek, which he named Denver City in honor of the governor of the Kansas Territory, James W. Denver (**at right**, in a portrait by Whitehurst Studio, c1856). What he didn't

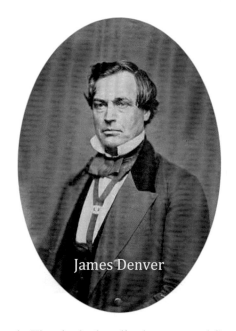

James Denver

know was that Governor Denver had resigned that same month. The site had earlier been named St. Charles, and Larimer's son William persuaded the residents to go along with the change.

William Larimer

Larimer (**at left**, in an unattributed image) was born to wealthy farmers in Westmoreland County, Pennsylvania. As a young man he started a business hauling rocks for the new Pennsylvania Turnpike. He then opened a mercantile and began to freight goods between Pittsburgh and Philadelphia. An astute businessman, he founded the Westmoreland Coal Company and eventually became the first president of the Pittsburgh and Connellsville Railroad. He was the treasurer of the Ohio and Pennsylvania Railroad and the Remington Coal railroad. In 1852 he was given an honorary rank of major general in the Pennsylvania State Militia.

A supporter of women's rights, Larimer crusaded against both alcohol and slavery, the latter leading him to a long friendship with newspaper editor and abolitionist Horace Greeley, the founder and editor of the *New York Tribune*. That was the most influential and powerful newspaper in the country until 1880, and it was decidedly biased toward a liberal agenda. A Republican, Greeley opposed the re-election of President Grant whom he viewed as overly conservative.

In a minor recession during 1854, which was particularly hard on railroad stocks, Larimer's fortunes declined. Typical of his personality, he packed up his family and moved out West to seek a new fortune. In 1855 he was one of the founders of La Platte, Nebraska (just south of Omaha), and then successfully campaigned for a seat in the Nebraska Legislature (1855-6). But a politician's paycheck couldn't support his large family, so they moved to Leavenworth, Kansas two years later. There, he learned of a gold strike near Pike's Peak and that fall (1858) he led a small expedition to investigate and assess the potential of the area.

In late November, they arrived at Cherry Creek. Along with Folsom Dorsett, M.M. Jewett, C.A. Lawrence and Richard E. Whitsett (all of Leavenworth), Larimer and his son William staked out a square mile of land, using logs as markers. The property was not legally

Above: Horace Greeley, in a Schlegel litho of a Frank Koss engraving, c.1870. (Henry Schile registered the original copyright.)

open to settlement (that didn't happen until 1861), but Larimer went ahead and built a cabin, which he claimed was the first permanent home in the future city of Denver (on the southwest corner of Larimer Street and 15th Street). However, a reproduction of an 1858 painting by A.H. Barker (below), copyrighted in 1888, claims to show the first house in Denver, which Barker said he built at the corner of Wynkoop and 12th Street.

THE FIRST HOUSE IN DENVER.
After Commencement of Official Survey, Nov. 1st 1858, corner Wynkoop and 12th Sts.

The first cabin in the future city of Denver was erected in 1858, but there is some controversy about who built it.

That winter, Larimer and his partners worked furiously platting and laying out streets, commercial zones and residential lots.

Then, everything fell into place in May when John H. Gregory of Cherokee County, Georgia, discovered gold in a gulch off the Vasquez Fork of the South Platte. The site, called Gregory Diggings, was about forty miles west of fledgling Denver. Larimer's friend Horace Greeley, along with Henry Villard of the *Cincinnati Daily Commercial* and A.D. Richardson of the *Boston Journal* all visited the site and spread the word. The boom was on! The new city took root and grew at an astounding rate.

By that Christmas, there was a bank, a stage depot (residents donated 53 city lots to make it happen), a mercantile and saloons, along with dozens of homes and temporary structures. The *Rocky Mountain News* also started publishing in 1859. Its publisher was William Byers and the paper lasted until 2009. A second town was established between the Gregory Diggings and Denver in June 1859, and named Golden after one of the original miners, Tom Golden.

On February 28, 1861, the Colorado Territory was organized and signed into existence by President James Buchanan. The capital was located in Colorado City (1861–63), then Golden City (1863–69), and finally in Denver City (1869–76). Colorado Territory (which succeeded the short-lived provisional Territory of Jefferson, 1860-1861) had the same boundaries as the current State of Colorado.

Larimer became a judge and in 1862 he formed the Colorado 3rd Volunteers. He was planning on serving at the rank of colonel, but was blocked by the new (second) Governor, John Evans, so he returned to Kansas and raised four companies where he served as a captain until 1865. After the war, he was elected as a state senator in Kansas for three years. He died on the family farm in 1875.

John Evans

Governor Evans (**at right**, unattributed, c1850) was a medical doctor, a railroad stockholder and one of the founders of Northwestern University and also the University of Denver. He graduated from Cincinnati College's medical school in 1838, and was one of the founders of Lakeside Hospital (later Mercy) in Chicago. He governed approximately 50,000 residents. The official Census in 1860 was 34,277 but estimates are that some 15,000 miners in the far reaches of the mountains were not included. Evans had succeeded William Gilpin as Territorial Governor. Gilpin served one year, after which a financial scandal ruined his reputation. He went on to become a very successful land speculator in New Mexico, where his ethics again were questionable.

In the early 1860s, growth hit a plateau for a while when the easiest gold (placer deposits) began to run out and the miners didn't have the right equipment to go after deeper veins. But progress continued nonetheless, and the city was officially incorporated on November 7, 1861.

In March of 1862, the Civil War came to Colorado. Early that year the Confederacy claimed southern New Mexico as its territory and, with diminishing resources, had an eye on the gold deposits in Colorado.

The Confederate General Henry Sibley (**at right**, c1863) had defeated a Union force under the command of Colonel Edward Canby in February at Valverde, New Mexico, and had seized Santa Fe on March 10th. He then sent 250 Texan troops through the Glorieta Pass, which would open the way to the Raton Pass and the high plains. But Union forces marched down from Denver over Raton and arrived at Glorieta Pass in time to repulse the invaders.

Major John M. Chivington (**below**, unattributed) distinguished himself on the Union side during the battle, including destroying the enemy's supply train, but his actions were later questioned. There is evidence that he took some persuading to attack the supply train even though it was virtually unguarded, and that the

Henry Sibley

attack was not his idea, but the suggestion of Jim Collins, a BIA official who served under Chivington. The Major was also

Chivington

accused of delaying ordering his men to support Col. John P. Slough of the 1st Colorado Infantry earlier in the battle, and of disobeying an order to flank the enemy which would probably have ended the engagement sooner.

In all about 1,300 Union soldiers and 1,100 Confederates participated in the engagement. The end result was that the Confederate force returned to Texas and the south gave up its plans to seize the Colorado goldfields.

Not everyone in Colorado favored entering the war. William Cornell Jewett (**at right**), a native of New York, had settled near Pike's Peak and appeared as a delegate at a Colorado peace convention in 1861. Over the next four years he made several trips to Europe in an effort to gain overseas support to end the war. He eventually became known as 'Colorado Jewett', and in 1864 he attempted to negotiate a settlement by inviting leaders from both sides to a conference in Niagara Falls. A voice of reason in an age of madness, Jewett was appalled at the numbers of casualties. *The New York Times* has estimated that as many as 750,000 soldiers died in the four years of the war – twelve times the cost in U.S. lives during two decades of conflict in Vietnam, and almost twice the entire American losses in World War II. (There is a golf course in Colorado Springs that was founded by a Bill Jewett of Long Island who owned the New London gold mine in Alma, Colorado and who moved here in 1898. We were unable to ascertain whether the two Bill Jewetts, both from New York, and both residents of the Colorado Springs area, were related.)

Colorado's William Jewett campaigned with great dignity and fervor to end the Civil War. (Brady-Handy c1861)

The Confederacy wasn't only after gold in Colorado, and in that it was prescient. The state would eventually become a major supplier of minerals and metals for American industry. Since the Civil War, mining in Colorado has produced aluminum (bauxite), beryllium, chromium, coal, copper, gemstones, gold, iron, lead, manganese, mercury, molybdenum, nickel, phosphorus, silica, silver, sodium, sulfur, tin, titanium, tungsten, uranium, vanadium and zinc.

In the wake of the battle at Glorieta Pass in March of 1862, the United States Army commissioned the Fort Collins Military Reservation that summer. The fort was also intended to protect stage lines from attacks by Cheyenne and Arapaho forces. Its establishment was one element in an escalation that led to the Colorado War, a two-year conflict from 1863 to 1865 that eventually embroiled the Lakota (Sioux), Comanche and Kiowa nations.

Above is a photograph of the Southern Plains delegation, taken in the White House Conservatory on March 27, 1863. *"The interpreter William Simpson Smith and the agent Samuel G. Colley are standing at the left of the group; the white woman standing at the far right is often identified as Mary Todd Lincoln. The Indians in the front row are, left to right: War Bonnet, Standing in the Water, and Lean Bear of the Cheyennes, and Yellow Wolf of the Kiowas. Yellow Wolf is wearing the Thomas Jefferson peace medal that aroused such interest. The identities of the Indians of the second row are unknown. Within eighteen months from the date of this sitting, all four men in the front row were dead. Yellow Wolf died of pneumonia a few days after the picture was taken; War Bonnet and Standing in the Water died in the Sand Creek Massacre; and Lean Bear was killed by troops from Colorado Territory who mistook him for a hostile."*

(Source: Diplomats in Buckskin by Herman J. Viola, p. 101. Photo by Matthew Brady.)

It's not surprising that Yellow Wolf's medal was an issue of interest, as the Lewis and Clark expedition had presented it to a member of his family. Two centuries after the Corps of Discovery, in November of 2003, another man of the same name addressed an audience at the U.S. Mint during the unveiling of the 2004 nickel: "My tribal name is Yellow Wolf, pronounced Zaa-shaa-shee-dish in my native language" said Gerard Baker of the National Park Service. He is a full blood member of the Mandan-Hidatsa Tribe of the Fort Berthold Reservation in Mandaree, North Dakota. "My family own(s) an original peace medal of Thomas Jefferson... It still means peace, unity and friendship. What it means the most to us, and what it should mean the most to all of us, is the understanding and willingness to learn. And the willingness to remember who we are, so that we never lose who we are..."

There was a lot of military experience available to the Governor of Colorado during the engagements of 1863 to 1865. Although he was not involved, many seasoned field commanders such as Brevet Brigadier General John E. Cummins (above, commander of the 8th Volunteer Infantry in Ohio) were moving West after mustering out. Cummins retired to Denver shortly after this photograph was made, where he died in 1875 at just 44 years of age.

(Matthew Brady, c1865: Liljenquist Family Collection of Civil War Photographs)

While his sentiments are admirable, the sad truth is that Western expansion, the doctrine of Manifest Destiny, almost completely destroyed a number of Native cultures. The Colorado War was undertaken as an effort to defend settlers and travelers from aggression, but it culminated in the most shameful and ugly event in the State's otherwise very admirable history, the Sand Creek Massacre.

The U.S. Army actually played quite a small role in the war. Militia, including the infamous Third Colorado Cavalry, primarily conducted operations.

This was an outfit comprised of 100-day volunteers that, on November 29th 1864, attacked and destroyed a peaceful village of Cheyenne and Arapaho.

In 1851 the United States and seven Native nations had concluded the Treaty of Fort Laramie, which recognized Native ownership of what is now southeast Wyoming, eastern Colorado, southwest Nebraska and western Kansas. After the gold rush, the government decided to revisit that. In 1861, the Southern Cheyenne and Arapaho signed the Treaty of Fort Wise, the terms of which ceded most of the Native territory (about 92%) to the United States. What was left was a patch in eastern Colorado stretching from the Arkansas to Sand Creek. However, many of the Cheyenne either knew nothing of the Fort Wise agreement, or they disagreed with it. They continued hunting buffalo throughout their former lands, which were now being traversed and even settled by ever larger numbers of European settlers and miners.

Not all of the Natives were opposed to the Treaty. In late November Black Kettle's band of about 800 Southern Cheyenne joined with Niwot's small band of Arapaho in a camp along the Sand Creek, and Black Kettle flew an American flag over his tent as a sign to the Army that the band was peaceful. When most of the men left the village to hunt buffalo, 700 militia of the 1st and 3rd Colorado Cavalry, under John Chivington (who, incidentally, was an ordained minister) approached. When Chivington gave the order to attack, two of his officers – Captain Silas Soule and Lieutenant Joseph Cramer – refused and ordered their men to step down. The rest of the Cavalry force immediately set to and massacred everyone they could find, including dozens of children. They then mutilated the bodies in an orgy of bloodletting, cutting people to pieces, scalping them, beating their brains out, cutting off fingers and ears for the jewelry and mutilating and removing their private parts. Sorting through various accounts, the report of trader George Bent (son of William Bent of Bent's Fort) who was in the camp and survived, seems to be a reasonable estimate of the carnage: 137 people were killed, 28 men and 109 women and children. Bent and two women in the camp survived, along with a few who fled to a neighboring Cheyenne village. Twenty-four soldiers died, many possibly from friendly fire as there had been quite a bit of alcohol consumed before the massacre.

Lt. Col. Samuel S.F. Tappan, 1st Colorado Regt. of Volunteers, gave testimony to the Congressional investigation that supported evidence given by survivors regarding the atrocities committed by the Reverend Chivington and his men.

(Unattributed photograph.)

A United States Congressional Committee looking into the massacre discovered that Chivington and his men decorated their weapons and hats with scalps and other body parts, including human fetuses and male and female genitalia. They later paraded their gruesome trophies through the streets of Denver, including impromptu rallies at saloons and even one in the Apollo Theater.

The Committee said of Chivington: "he deliberately planned and executed a foul and dastardly massacre which would have disgraced the verist savage among those who were the victims of his cruelty. Having full knowledge of their friendly character, having himself been instrumental to some extent in placing them in their position of fancied security, he took advantage of their in-apprehension and defenceless condition to gratify the worst passions that ever cursed the heart of man."

Among the dead at Sand Creek were War Bonnet and Standing in the Water, both of whom had visited the White House in late March of the previous year. Although the government signed a reparations measure called the Treaty of the Little Arkansas in 1865, promising more freedom to the Nations for hunting and certain awards to the families of the survivors, that was replaced by the Medicine Lodge Treaties in 1867 which relocated the Kiowa, Comanche, Apache, Southern Cheyenne and Arapaho to Kansas and Oklahoma.

Red Cloud

The Comanche chief Ten Bears summarized the treaties thus:

"You said that you wanted to put us upon reservation, to build our houses and make us medicine lodges. I do not want them. I was born on the prairie where the wind blew free and there was nothing to break the light of the sun. I was born where there were no inclosures [sic] and where everything drew a free breath. I want to die there and not within walls. I know every stream and every wood between the Rio Grande and the Arkansas. I have hunted and lived over the country. I lived like my fathers before me, and like them, I lived happily."

The Northern Cheyenne did not participate in the Medicine Lodge Treaties. They instead remained with the Lakota in resistance, following the leadership of Red Cloud (**at right**, c.1880 in an unattributed portrait), and fought on in the Powder River country.

The citizens of Denver had other things on their minds in the spring of 1864. That May, Cherry Creek flooded. The creek had not been highly regarded until this time, as there was rarely a strong flow and the bed was, more often than not, completely dry. Indeed, many of the wooden buildings and homes in the city were built along its banks. The Arapaho had warned the residents not to build in or near the creek, but nobody listened. The flood took between 15 and 20 lives.

(Photo by George D. Wakely, 1864)

In 1865, John Evans was invited by the new President of the United States to resign as a consequence of the Sand Creek Massacre. Andrew Johnson succeeded Abraham Lincoln in April, and within ninety days he fired Governor Evans. The replacement, appointed on October 17th, was Alexander Cummings, a native of Williamsport, Pennsylvania. Cummings was a Republican, Andrew Johnson was a Democrat even though he was Lincoln's Vice President, and of course Lincoln himself was a Whig from 1834 to 1854, a Republican from 1854 to 1865, and a National Union Party member in 1864 and 1865. (The latter was a Republican device to attract hawkish, pro-war Democratic votes during the election of 1864, and it seemingly worked.) The concept of putting the people before the party has been largely lost in modern politics.

During 1865, the first steps in Johnson's Reconstruction plan were being implemented. None of the Southern states granted voting rights to black men, and voters in Connecticut, Wisconsin, Minnesota and the Territory of Colorado also rejected the reform that year. In fact, the Colorado initiative specifically excluded African Americans, Native Americans, people of Asian descent and all women. Four years later, on December 10th 1869, neighboring Wyoming would be the first Territory or state to approve universal suffrage for women. There had been partial concessions: Women in New Jersey who could prove that they had $250 had the right to vote from 1776 until 1807, and Kentucky allowed women to vote in school board elections from 1837 until 1902, a boon that was also granted in Kansas in 1861. It wasn't until November 7th, 1893 that Colorado's men finally passed a referendum giving their wives, daughters and mothers a say in governing themselves. Incredibly, Colorado was only the third state to grant voting rights to women (Utah did so in 1870, and amended its Constitution in 1895 to grant women full suffrage). Idaho followed suit in 1896. On August 26th 1920, a constitutional amendment was adopted (after Tennessee ratified it on August 18, thereby becoming the necessary thirty-sixth state to do so). The Nineteenth Amendment prohibits any U.S. citizen from being denied the right to vote on the basis of sex.

Natalie Gray of Colorado Springs was a member of the National Woman's Party. She was arrested Aug. 17, 1917 and spent thirty days in the Occaquan workhouse for picketing the White House.

(Photo by Harris & Ewing, Inc., 1916)

Kit Carson

For most of his life Christopher 'Kit' Carson was an upstanding person. In his early years he was diligent and courageous, and of impeccable character. His word was iron, he didn't drink or curse, and he relied on nobody to carry his load. He was born on Christmas Eve, 1809, in Kentucky, the eleventh of fifteen children. Carson grew up in Missouri, where his neighbors were the children and grandchildren of Daniel Boone. His father died in a farm accident, felling trees, when Kit was eight. To help support the family he quit school and took up hunting, and saddle making. Not at all comfortable with that latter apprenticeship, he joined a wagon train in his mid-teens and headed west, bound for Santa Fe. Carson spent the next few years doing menial work in Taos, but while there he learned Spanish and several Native languages. He picked up the rudiments of trapping from an old family friend, Matt Kinkead, who lived in Taos. At age 19 he was hired as part of a group of forty or

Kit Carson

so men to trap fur between New Mexico and California, under the leadership of Ewing Young. On the return trip, they worked the country along the Colorado River.

From then until 1840, when he was 31 years old, Carson trapped extensively through the Rockies and the Sierras. Along the way he first married an Arapaho bride, and later a Cheyenne woman. The former, Waa Nibe, he met at a mountain man rendezvous on the Green River in western Wyoming, and he fought a duel to win her. They had one daughter, Adeline, and Waa Nibe died in childbirth (probably in 1838). Carson married his second wife in 1841 but she left him almost immediately to live with her family rather than roam the country.

With the advent of silk hats, the need for furs dissipated quickly and Carson moved to Colorado to find work. He spent a year or so working as a hunter supplying William Bent's original fort with buffalo, deer and other game. In 1842, he brought Adeline back to his family in Missouri, and on his way back to Colorado he met John Frémont on a steamboat in St. Louis.

Josefa Jaramillo, Kit Carson's third wife who was 14 at the time they married. He was 33. They had eight children and eventually lived near Fort Lyons, Colorado, where he died in 1868. (Unattributed. C.1844)

Frémont was 29 at the time, Carson was 33, and they struck up a friendship. It didn't take much to persuade Carson to sign on as a guide for Frémont's first expedition through the mountains. The goal was to explore ways through the Rockies so that trade routes and eventually railroads could create economic ties between California and the United States. This was the first of several expeditions that led through Colorado to points west, and Frémont's published journals of their five-month adventure began to create a heroic persona for Carson in Eastern newspapers, periodicals and dime novels.

On his return, Carson married his third wife, fourteen-year-old Josefa Jaramillo, the daughter of a wealthy Taos merchant (**at left**). To do so he became a Catholic, which was not so very much out of character for him. At this time Carson was a serious and still highly moral person. The union was a success, and produced eight children.

In 1843, Frémont and Carson teamed up again for an expedition to map the western half of the Oregon Trail from South Pass in Wyoming to the Pacific Ocean. Some violent encounters with Natives on this journey began to earn Carson a reputation as a somewhat ruthless Indian fighter.

On a third expedition in 1845, Frémont began to exhibit a more erratic persona, and Carson's personality certainly became more judgmental, harsh and unforgiving. At one point, Frémont almost goaded a Mexican general into a fight that would have wiped out his own party (General Castro had far superior forces). Then they got into a couple of small battles with Native warriors shortly thereafter, on the shores of Upper Klamath Lake. The lake is on the California-Oregon border, about 200 miles inland from the Pacific. In retaliation for a night attack on their party, Frémont and Carson led a brutal assault on what was probably an uninvolved nearby village, killing fourteen people. The night before, one of the attackers had been killed and Carson had mutilated his face in a fit of fury, slamming it beyond recognition with the butt of a gun.

On June 28th, Carson murdered three peaceful Mexican nationals near San Francisco on Frémont's orders. The expedition had now become part of the Mexican-American War, after Frémont had helped to instigate a revolt by American settlers in southern California (the Bear Flag Revolt).

Through 1846, Carson served in the war with Mexico, acquitting himself well in the fight for California. He was made a lieutenant in Commodore Robert Field Stockton's battalion. On one occasion, he and a couple of other volunteers worked their way through enemy lines to summon relief for General Stephen Kearney's forces under siege near San Pasqual. The nearest available garrison was at San Diego, so the three ran south down the coast at night, some twenty-four miles, barefoot so their boots wouldn't make noise.

Robert Stockton

At the end of the conflict, Stockton (**at left**, c.1867, Brady-Handy Collection) appointed Frémont governor of California. Carson and Josefa moved to a ranch near Taos in 1849. Between then and March of 1854, he acted as a scout for the Army who were fighting an ongoing war with the Jicarilla Apaches.

In 1854, Carson was appointed as the Indian agent for the Ute and Apache tribes near Taos. At the outbreak of the Civil War in 1861, he resigned that post and began training volunteers. He and his recruits saw action at the Battle of Valverde in 1862 and, after the Confederate forces retired to Texas, Carson entered a new war. Many of the Navajo refused to move to the reservation, and Carson was hired to force them to comply. He employed a limited version of the tactics Maj. Gen. William Tecumseh Sherman would use two years later when he marched through Georgia to the sea. Carson burned Navajo crops, destroyed methods of trade, stole cattle and in general implemented a scorched earth policy. The Navajos' traditional enemies, the smaller Ute, Pueblo, Hopi, and Zuni tribes soon joined him in his efforts. In 1864, roughly 8,000 Navajo surrendered and the Army walked them 300 grueling desert miles to a new reservation near Fort Sumner (Bosque Redondo). The event is still known as The Long Walk in Navajo culture. The death toll was somewhere between 236 and 2,000 people (depending on who is recounting the story), most of them from heat exhaustion and starvation.

Two years later, the Navajo were returned to the Arizona-New Mexico border because the land around Fort Sumner couldn't feed them. By then, Carson had moved to Colorado.

But back in 1864, Carson had been sent to Texas to take on the Kiowa, Comanche, and Apache resistance. At the head of 400 troops he lost a battle to the combined Native forces at Adobe Walls, and made an orderly retreat.

In October of 1865, he was promoted to brigadier general and in 1866 was appointed commandant of Ft. Garland, Colorado. The fort was close to what is now the Colorado-New Mexico line, halfway across the state, and it had been established in 1858 to protect settlers in the San Luis Valley from Ute raids. Carson had many Ute friends and helped bring some order to the area. While commandant of the post, and through the next year when he was mustered out of the army, he worked a ranch by Boggsville, near the confluence of the Purgatoire and Arkansas Rivers in southeastern Colorado.

It was about this time that Carson first saw himself featured in dime novels, and he was quite uncomfortable with the heroic status attributed to him.

In 1867, Kit Carson escorted a Ute delegation to Washington to visit President Andrew Johnson, and returned to Colorado just in time to see his wife, Josefa, die after a difficult delivery as she gave him their eighth child. She was only 39. Broken-hearted and in poor health himself, he went under the care of a Dr. Tilton at nearby Fort Lyons. He had an abdominal aortic aneurysm, which ruptured on the 23rd of May and caused his passing at age 58. Kit Carson is buried beside his wife, in Taos. There is a town in Cheyenne County, and a county in Colorado named after him.

Seven years after Carson's tenure as commander, photographer Tim O'Sullivan took this image of the main entrance to Fort Garland, Colorado. He was attached to Lieutenant George Wheeler's 1874 expedition that explored the country west of the 100th Meridian. Note the crow's nest flagpole that allowed a man to be lifted high to keep watch.

Chapter 4
The Railroads Arrive

The 1860s witnessed the beginning of railroads in Colorado. With the Union Pacific running through Cheyenne just 100 miles north of Denver, mining and ranching interests in the Territory saw an opportunity to reach markets on both sides of the continent. While stagecoaches did a fair job of carrying people, and mule trains handled freight, only a railroad could transform the Territory into an organized, affluent state of the Union. The coach shown **above** is the Overland from Hays, Kansas to Denver, in an 1867 Alexander Gardner photograph. (It's interesting that just two years after the war, everyone on the roof, including the driver and the soldier riding shotgun, is African American.)

Horse-drawn wagons and coaches had been used in Europe for centuries, and in Greece for at least four thousand years. Steam locomotives weren't all that new either. The first commercial railroads had appeared in Britain back in 1825, and in the United States in 1827. The issue wasn't technology: it was the terrain. Driving a wagon across the prairie was a lot different than driving one deep into the Rockies to an isolated mining camp. And while a team of horses can follow a mountain track, trains have great difficulty ascending even the gentlest of slopes because of the lack of traction between their steel wheels on a steel track. As about half of Colorado is mountainous (more than fifty peaks in the state reach above 14,000 feet), and almost all of the mines were located in the mountains or the foothills, building relatively level railroad beds through this terrain was incredibly daunting. Even if one could find a route between the crags, there are countless streams and creeks to cross, plus four major rivers that rise in the Rockies – the mighty Colorado, the Rio Grande, the Platte and the Arkansas. Virtually none of the waterways are navigable.

Above, a stagecoach is about to leave the Holladay Overland Mail & Express Company in Denver.
(Unattributed, 1867)

In the 1850s there was a lot of discussion among Denver businessmen about the possibility of wooing the transcontinental railroad through the city, and some corporations were formed to do just that, but they made no progress. Two Acts of Congress in 1862 and 1864 provided a contractual basis for the Union Pacific to gain the necessary right-of-way to construct a line from Omaha as far west as was feasible, with the route lying across the high plains of southern Wyoming. The deal was supported with land grants and a charter to issue public bond sales to raise capital. Construction actually began in 1863, but by the end of the war only forty miles of track had been laid. Colorado politicians and businessmen were encouraged by the fact that they had not yet been bypassed, and they made several efforts to find a route through the Rockies that would bring trains to Denver.

Placer gold deposits are small amounts of the metal that reside in gravel or sand, usually in the path of a stream or glacier that has exposed them and severed them from the lode, or main ore vein. As gold is very heavy, it generally just lies where it falls in the water and doesn't get washed away. The word is pronounced 'plasser', and is derived from the Spanish word *placel*, which was a Catalan term meaning something along the lines of 'banks of sand or rocks in the sea'.

In the early 1860s, Colorado's economy was less than exuberant, in large part because easy to recover placer gold deposits were running out. The initial phase of mining, where a single man could stake a claim and find ore, was about done. It was time for professional corporations with experience in extracting ore from solid rock to take over. The problem was that the machinery to do so, and the quantities of rock that needed to be moved both relied on railroads. Horse teams simply couldn't handle the weight.

In 1864 the Army established a small fort called Camp Rankin in the extreme northeast corner of Colorado, about a mile from the stagecoach stop (and Pony Express station in 1860-61) at Julesburg. The fort, renamed Fort Sedgwick in 1866, was located at the confluence of Lodgepole Creek and the South Platte River. Jules Beni, who had been an employee of the Overland stage company, named the town sometime prior to 1858. Beni was a crook whose gang was robbing the stages, and when the company replaced him he attempted to ambush his replacement, Jack Slade. There is some evidence that the ambush was their second encounter, and that Beni had seriously wounded Slade in a gunfight earlier. The day of the ambush on Slade's ranch, Beni was captured, tied to a fencepost and shot several times. Slade then cut off his ears for a souvenir.

Above: Major General John Sedgwick, the highest-ranking Union casualty in the Civil War, who led a campaign against the Cheyenne in 1857. (Brady?)

At right: A plaque erected by the Julesburg Historical Society in 1940 reads... "Due South 1¼ miles is the site of Fort Sedgwick established in September, 1864, as a United States Army post called Camp Rankin and Post Julesburg. Name changed in November 1865, to honor General John Sedgewick who was killed at Spottsylvania May 9, 1864. The fort protected the stage line and emigrant trains from Indians. Abandoned in May, 1871. From this fort, Sedgwick County derives its name. Erected by the State Historical Society of Colorado from the Mrs. J.N. Hall Foundation."

On January 7, 1865, about one thousand Lakota, Southern Cheyenne and Arapaho warriors attacked the town and defeated a small force of soldiers who took refuge, with the remaining civilians, inside the fort. The attack was a direct response to news of the Sand Creek Massacre. The same Native war party returned a month later and burned the town, leaving the fort alone.

In June of 1867, the Union Pacific line reached Julesburg. In all, there were nine miles of railroad in Colorado, because the line barely dipped into the state from Nebraska, and then left again. That November, former Governor John Evans led a group of businessmen in the formation of the Denver Pacific, which was created to connect Denver to the UP line in Cheyenne. In 1869, the Denver Pacific received a land grant from Congress, and that spring began grading. In June, the UP linked up with the Central Pacific in Utah, completing the first transcontinental railroad (actually, it only ran from the Sacramento River to the Missouri, where it linked up with other lines).

When the UP decided not to lay track over their graded route, the Denver group formed an alliance with the Kansas Pacific. One advantage to this arrangement was that a second line was started from Kansas City toward Denver. Both lines were made operable in 1870, completing the first ocean-to-ocean continuous line. The image at left was published the next year, and it illustrates that buffalo were still quite plentiful on the plains east of the Rockies. Note the large spark-arresting smokestack on the wood-burning locomotive, designed to avoid setting the prairie on fire. That September, a coalition of the UP and business interests in Golden completed a connecting line from Golden to Denver.

An 1871 print from Frank Leslie's illustrated newspaper (v. 32, no. 818) shows hunters shooting buffalo on the line of the Kansas-Pacific Railroad.

A Hill in the Mountains

With the decline in placer gold finds, miners had begun to dig into rock-bound veins of gold below the surface. However, sulphides surrounded much of the trapped ore. This was a problem because of the way in which they were extracting the ore from the rocks. They began by crushing the rock with stamp mills (essentially, huge iron hammers), and then washing the dust across copper/mercury plates. The gold would form a compound (an amalgam) with the mercury, the dust was washed away, and the final step in smelting was to release the gold from the mercury. This was done in small volume by forcing it through a chamois (leather) filter. The mercury would pass through and the gold would remain behind. A more industrial method was to heat the compound in a retort, and allow the mercury to evacuate as vapor. (In small batches, miners would use potatoes to catch the mercury vapor.)

Nathaniel Hill

A strong sulphide presence can make the extraction process quite difficult, and a lot less efficient. Sulphides simply wouldn't give up their bond. A lot of gold was washing away with the cleansing water.

Enter Mr. Hill.

A New Yorker by birth, Nathaniel Peter Hill, (**at left** in an 1875 Matthew Brady portrait) graduated from Brown University in Rhode Island in 1856 with a degree in chemistry. He spent the next eight years on the faculty at Brown, and was instrumental in introducing the concept of experimental laboratories on campus. In 1865, he spent some time traveling in Colorado, investigating the supply and properties of various minerals, and became enamored with the countryside. He also watched miners smelting gold, and he began to buy some claims. It didn't take Hill long to work out that the stamp mills in the mines that he bought were resoundingly inefficient. So that fall he crossed the Atlantic, and then spent several months in England and Germany learning about the extraction of metals from sulphides and similar compounds. In the simplest terms, what he learned was that copper could be used to extract gold.

Back in Colorado, Hill struck up a friendship with the industrialist James Lyon. In partnership with Henry Pullman (the sleeping car manufacturer), Lyon had built a smelter in the area known as Black Hawk in 1865. It was downstream from the spot where John Gregory had discovered gold in a gulch off the Vasquez Fork of the South Platte (forty miles west of Denver). Using old technology, the smelter had failed. But with Lyon's encouragement and hard-earned wisdom, financial backing from back East, and the knowledge that Hill had gained in Europe, he founded the very successful Boston & Colorado Smelting Company in 1868.

Hill's smelter rejuvenated gold mining and reignited interest in the establishment of railroads to support the industry. Then, the following year major silver deposits were discovered in Boulder Canyon and several other regions south and west of there. Within five years, silver was producing even more revenue than gold. The Colorado economy was firing on all cylinders again.

Nathaniel Hill was elected mayor of Black Hawk in 1871, and served in the territorial government the next two years. In 1873, he moved the smelting operation to Denver where he eventually ran for and was elected as a United States senator (1879-1885). He died on May 22, 1900.

Morrison (above) was named after stonemason George Morrison who was instrumental in bringing the Denver, South Park & Pacific Railroad to town in 1874.
(W.G. Chamberlain, 1878)

In the fall of 1870, ex-Union General William Jackson Palmer and former territorial governor A. Cameron Hunt formed a new company called the Denver & Rio Grande. It began life at a time when the country was descending into a recession, and when railroads were no longer receiving land grants (the Denver Pacific had been the only Colorado-owned or based line to do so). Palmer raised funds in Europe and in 1871 began building the country's first narrow gauge track (rails laid 3 feet apart, as opposed to the standard gauge of 4 foot 8-1/2 inches). Shorter ties, lighter rails and smaller locomotives and rolling stock made it less expensive to build. Plus, the route was relatively flat for Colorado, stretching from Denver through Colorado Springs (which the D&RG had actually founded), and on to Santa Fe. In 1872 it reached Pueblo, and that year the line also installed the first air brakes in American freight locomotives. The following year, the recession hit and construction was interrupted, but in 1874 surveyors for the company did find coal near Trinidad. The line reached there two years later.

Views like this one of the Garden of the Gods (now a public park and a registered National Natural Landmark in Colorado Springs) were published by Byron Gurnsey the year the line opened in 1871, or very shortly thereafter, to promote tourism.

The first railroads to penetrate the Front Range and reach the mines were lines to Black Hawk and Morrison. In 1872 the Colorado Central laid track from Golden to the smelter in Black Hawk, and the following year extended service to the coal reserves of Boulder Valley and almost all the way to Longmont. 1872 also saw the emergence of the new company, the Denver, South Park & Pacific. It laid track to Morrison (see previous page), and then ran out of funds during a recession that would last the next several years.

Ironically, the recession was triggered by the bankruptcy of Jay Cooke, the largest stockholder in the Northern Pacific. One of the most significant advances made in 1873 was a small gain by a new

player, the Atchison, Topeka and Santa Fe, which constructed a mere ten miles of track from the Kansas state line into Colorado before running out of money, too. As the economy recovered, so did faith in the enterprise and the AT&SF reached Pueblo in 1876.

The national economy played a major role in the way almost all of the early railroads were financed. Located literally at the edge of the country and remote in every aspect, these small lines had

This illustration from Frank Leslie's Illustrated Newspaper on October 4th, 1873 shows crowds in the street at the beginning of the financial panic (which actually had occurred on September 19th). The location is the intersection of Nassau and Broad Streets with Wall Street, and the building in the center is the Jay Cooke & Co. Bank. Mr. Cooke was the main investor in the Northern Pacific Railroad, and his personal bankruptcy was in large part because of over-investing in an effort to bring a transcontinental railroad to Duluth, Minnesota from the Pacific. He was also involved in a financial scandal that caused Canadian Prime Minister Sir John MacDonald to lose the 1873 election. Cooke again became rich late in the decade through his involvement with a silver mine in Utah.

difficulty raising the financing needed for a first-rate railroad. Track installations were done on a shoestring (ironically, they were called 'placer' roads), with built-in obsolescence that would hopefully survive a full decade. The idea was that mine profits would support upgrading the track, sleepers, switches and other equipment as ore extraction increased. Some lines would also have to be moved, to change their steep grades and sharp turns as money became available to blast rock and carve a better, safer route. Derailments and wrecks were common: shipping goods and people was at least as risky as investing one's life savings in the companies. Nevertheless, there were plenty of railroad boosters, most of whom had some connection to the mines. One of the former was Jerome Chaffee, who addressed the Senate on the relationship between the Kansas Pacific and the Union Pacific in November 1877, and again in April 1878.

The Hon. J.B. Chaffee, Colorado's first U.S. Senator, in a c.1876 portrait (probably by Mathew B. Brady, and courtesy of the Brady-Handy collection at the Library of Congress). Chaffee was an early resident of Denver and contributed to the city's initial growth.

Chaffee and Teller

Chaffee was a U.S. Senator from Colorado, a mine owner and one of the founders of the First National Bank of Denver. He was born in upstate New York, near Buffalo, in 1825 and in his early twenties moved to Michigan and then Kansas, where he worked in a bank. In St. Joseph in 1859, he met his future partner Eben Smith, a miner who has enjoyed some considerable success in California. In 1860, Chaffee arrived in Colorado and the two opened a stamp mill in Lake Gulch that same year. They operated it for three years and sold it in 1863. The partners took the proceeds and bought the Bobtail Mine near Black Hawk, the Gregory Mine in Teller County and a few other smaller properties. In 1864, they sold almost all of their interests to a Rhode Island mining consortium. Chaffee went on to found the Little Pittsburg Consolidated Mining Company, and in 1865 he led a group that created the First National Bank, where he served as president until 1880. He was an early advocate of statehood for Colorado, helped organize the Colorado Territory, and served in its first legislature as speaker. He was the territorial delegate to the U.S. Congress, and represented the state as its first U.S. Senator from November 15, 1876 until March 3, 1879. The junior Senator was H.M. Teller, his cousin and also a Republican, but a political foe.

During his time in Washington, Chaffee opened up Colorado's San Juan mining district by engineering a treaty with the Ute nation that ceded part of their reservation, and he also directed legislation for a Congressionally approved national mining code. In 1884, Chaffee was elected state chairman of the Colorado Republican Party. Around that time, he became semi-retired from business and spent much of each year on the farm of his daughter Fannie Josephine, who was married to the son of President Grant, a friend of Chaffee's. He died at her Murryweather Farm in Westchester County, New York, near his birthplace, in 1886. Chaffee County in Colorado (established in 1879) is named after him.

Senator Henry Teller of Colorado served as a major general in the Colorado Militia from 1862-1864, and as Secretary of the Interior from 1882-85. Photo probably by Levin C. Handy, c.1876.

Henry Teller's first Senate term expired in 1882, but he returned to office from 1885 to 1909. A supporter of a silver standard (known as the Free Silver movement, as opposed to those who supported the traditional gold standard), he began life as a Republican but served from 1896 onward as a Democrat. In 1898 he sponsored an amendment to the joint resolution on the Spanish American War, a ten-week confrontation over independence on the island of Cuba, where American and Cuban forces prevailed. A successful businessman and hotelier, Teller was a champion of Native American land rights, saying that the federal policy of privatizing land ownership on reservations was a way "to despoil the Indians of their lands and to make them vagabonds on the face of the earth." The practice of allotment culminated in the Dawes Act of 1887, which essentially divided up tribal land into saleable small parcels, and then confiscated any land that wasn't allotted to a specific tribal member. Despite his efforts, allotment caused land ownership by Native Americans to decrease by more than 60% over the next half century. However Teller was also part of a movement to restrict Native religious and spiritual practices, and as Secretary of the Interior he appointed judges to prosecute immoral dancing (essentially, the Lakota Sun Dance), plural marriage and the sale of young women within a tribe for the purpose of marriage.

Jay Gould

No out-of-state investor had more influence on Colorado's emerging railroads than the controversial Jason Gould (shown at right in a late 1870s image from the Bain Collection). Gould was born to middle-class parents in Roxbury, New York in 1836 and began his working career as a bookkeeper in a forge. The blacksmith eventually offered him a partnership, which is indicative of the young man's presence and abilities. At the age of twenty, he started a tanning business in the northeast corner of Pennsylvania. The site would eventually become the town of Gouldsboro.

Jay Gould

Gould's first interest in railroads was the Rutland and Washington (based in Vermont), which was on the brink of bankruptcy during the panic of 1857. Gould picked it up for a dime on the dollar, and the road prospered during the Civil War years. In 1867 he became a director of the Erie Railroad and, during a battle for control of the company the following year, he went toe-to-toe with Cornelius Vanderbilt. To win, he issued fraudulent stock certificates, paid immense illegal bribes and generally showed himself to be ruthless and unscrupulous. He is often described as a robber baron. The following year (1869), he became infamous for almost cornering the gold market and causing the recession that began on Black Friday (Sept. 24, 1869). He was intimately involved with the questionable Tammany Hall political machine, and its notoriously corrupt leader, Boss Tweed.

After a scandal in the early 1870s that involved the Erie Railroad, a kidnapping and an international incident with Canada (and eventually cost him control of the Erie), Gould looked westward. A recession in 1873 allowed him to buy heavily in the Union Pacific and Missouri Pacific.

On June 21st, 1870, the Denver Pacific Railroad had reached the city of Denver, connecting via the UP line to Cheyenne. That August, the Kansas Pacific had connected Denver to Kansas City, Missouri, and the following month the Colorado Central Railroad connected Golden to Denver. The Kansas Pacific was the longest road in Colorado by the mid 1870s, but it didn't have a great financial foundation. The company controlled the Denver Pacific through a lease that also included coal rights through the Denver & Boulder Valley mine. The KP's physical structure was questionable, too. The lines were not in great shape, and this may have contributed to the company going into receivership. This allowed Gould to gain control. He then bought the Golden, Boulder & Caribou railroad and next concentrated on gaining control of the UP.

By 1879 that was accomplished, and by 1880 he had merged the KP, the DP, the D&BV, the GB&C and the Colorado Central with the UP. The bottom line of his involvement was that Denver, and not Golden, gained huge railroad access and the means to grow into the state's largest and most commercially viable city.

By 1882, Gould controlled one in every six miles of track in the United States. He governed the UP until 1883, three years after its merger with the Kansas Pacific, sold his stock for an immense fortune, and regained control of several smaller roads (including the Wabash and the Texas and Pacific) in the late 1880s. He also owned the Western Union Telegraph Company. Gould died in 1892 at the age of 56 from TB, and is buried at Woodlawn, in the Bronx.

Railroads brought everyday life with them. For example, in the spring of 1870, construction had begun about fifty miles east-southeast of downtown Denver on a Kansas Pacific station in the tiny hamlet of Deer Trail (now a stop on I-70). On July 4th the previous year, the community had hosted the first commercial rodeo in America (an event that still takes place today). The town is emblematic of myriad whistle-stops along the line, such as Limon, Agate (called Gebhard until 1882) or Strasburg (Comanche Crossing until 1875). Deer Trail grew quickly in the early years of railroading, but had some hard years during the Depression and absorbed an almost fatal blow during a flood in 1965. Today, the population is just 546 (2010 census). Thanks to Jay Gould, the Kansas Pacific had been consolidated with the Union Pacific in 1880. The line through Deer Trail still operates today.

Limon, just down the track, was apparently named after a supervisor on the railroad construction crew. The town earned notoriety in November 1900 when a young African American railroad worker, 16-year-old John Porter (aka Preston Porter Jr.) was burned at the stake for the murder and rape of an 11-year-old Caucasian girl, Louise Frost. The stake used was a railroad tie. Colorado has a strong history of lynchings (the word usually refers to hanging, but in fact covers all acts of mob justice that result in murder). Estimates are about 175, most of them to do with cattle rustling and horse thieving.

Thanks to the railroads, Colorado's population blossomed during the 1870s (growing 500%). Towns such as Colorado Springs owed their existence to the tracks, and Pueblo gained significantly from access to the bigger world. Greeley was built on land bought from the UP: it was the brainchild of the exotic and idealistic mind of Nathan Meeker, an editor at the New York Tribune who planned a farming community with 'high moral character' which he named after his publisher and friend, Horace Greeley.

Next page: the Colorado Central's Black Hawk bridge reaches across the main street,
in an 1881 photograph by Charles Weitfle.

The Denver & Rio Grande Expands

In June of 1872 the narrow gauge Denver & Rio Grande (D&RG) had reached Pueblo, and in 1876 the standard gauge Atchison, Topeka and Santa Fe Railway (AT&SF) arrived in the city. Both companies had plans on the Raton Pass, and the mines in western Colorado. In a race to start grading, some AT&SF engineers beat the competition and took possession of Raton Pass in the middle of a cold February night in 1878. The previous year, a smelter had been built in Leadville to process vast

deposits of silver, and the following year two more smelters followed. To take advantage of the boom, the two railway lines began to explore a route that followed the Arkansas River, which needed to navigate the narrow and dangerous Royal Gorge. Engineers from the AT&SF snuck up to the mouth of the canyon in an effort to repeat their success at Raton pass, but a crew from the D&RI outflanked them and set up camp inside the canyon itself.

Bat Masterson

The AT&SF hired the 25-year-old lawman William Barclay 'Bat' Masterson and a small army of mercenaries to fortify its position. Masterson (shown at right in a c.1915 Bain News Service image) had served as a sheriff's deputy in Dodge City in 1877, befriending another young deputy there named Wyatt Earp. He was the elected sheriff of Ford County, Kansas – a position he still held during the railroad incident. On returning to Kansas, he lost the next election in 1879.

In the Royal Gorge, with both camps armed to the teeth, widespread bloodshed was averted when both sides decided to fight it out in the courts. When that process slowed to a crawl, General William Jackson Palmer of the D&RG decided to solve the problem with force. He loaded a train in the yards in Denver with gunmen, and another in Pueblo, and the crews took each station along the way. Sometimes there was gunplay, and there were a couple of casualties, but the end of the confrontation was actually brought about in boardrooms. The AT&SF took the southern route through Raton Pass, and the D&RG, with Jay Gould and his deep pockets now on the Board, were free to build to Leadville. The Denver & Rio Grande would spend the next several years expanding in the west, following veins of silver, gold and lead.

After the conflict, Bat Masterson wandered through the West for a couple of years, making a meager living as a professional gambler. In 1881 he rejoined his friend Earp in Tombstone, and was hired to run the faro tables in the Earp brothers' saloon, the Oriental. After a brief visit and a gunfight in Dodge City in April of that year, Masterson became the marshal of Trinidad, Colorado, and then the Sheriff of South Pueblo.

Forty miles west of Denver, the town of Black Hawk nested below the Colorado Central line that connected it to Central City. Nathaniel Hill had built Colorado's first really successful ore smelter in Black Hawk in 1868, and the town eventually became known as the City of Mills. (Charles Weitfle, 1878)

Around that time he became a journalist, writing sports and editorial columns. He later moved to Denver, and in 1892 to the silver town of Creede. He died in New York in 1921 of a heart attack, just after completing his column for the *Morning Telegraph*. He was 67.

Shown is a stage emerging from a temporary tunnel on the Ouray-Red Mountain toll road in August of 1882. This road was used to haul ore from the mines, and the snow was from an avalanche the previous winter. (Moore Photo)

By 1880, Ouray had become a town of almost a thousand residents, the largest in the San Juan Mountains, because of silver. With the Utes on reservations since 1873, the country had become far less dangerous and there were new finds throughout the region. Camps had been established at Eureka, Gladstone and Mineral Point, and the mines needed rail support. That year, gold was discovered at Telluride, just southwest of Ouray.

In 1881, a new company was formed that was called the Denver & Rio Grande Western. With the same ownership and management, the new company began laying narrow gauge track from Salt Lake City toward Colorado. It met the Central Pacific in Ogden, playing into the nation's thirst for transcontinental lines. (By 1883, there were four of them – the Union Pacific, Southern Pacific, Northern Pacific and the AT&SF.) Although narrow gauge was more suited to the mountains because of low cost, tighter turning radii and better traction, the rest of the country was switching to standard gauge because of the increased freight capacity it offered. So, Palmer used standard length railroad ties and laid narrow gauge track most of the way, and dual gauge (a third rail that allowed the line to accommodate both gauges) where the lines interacted.

In southern Colorado, the D&RG changed the direction of its southbound route to west, and began extending lines toward Ouray and Silverton. Under the leadership of Alexander Hunt, engineers created switchbacks and tunnels to combat the grade. In many places, it requires two and even three miles of track to travel between two points a mile apart. The goal was a new railroad town being platted in the southern San Juans – Durango. Hunt's tracks reached the site in the summer of 1881, and then took a sharp right and headed north for Silverton. The line reached there the following summer (1882) and allowed ore to be shipped to Durango for smelting. Within three years, the population of Ouray doubled.

Chapter 5
From Territory To State

Twenty-five thousand people gathered at the 1907 State Fair in Pueblo. (Photo by Benjamin West Kilburn of New Hampshire)

In the summer of 1869, a horse exposition in Pueblo attracted almost two thousand attendees. Recognizing the benefits to the community, the event led to the first Southern Colorado Agricultural and Industrial Exposition on October 9th, 1872. It became the Colorado State Fair when it was incorporated on November 17, 1886. Today, the complex encloses just over 100 acres of land and fourteen permanent structures. Since 1903, the citizens of Colorado have funded it (at least in part). In 1917 the site was deeded to the state, and the organization received the State Fair Commission. Today it is known as the Colorado State Fair and Rodeo, which takes place near the end of August each summer. (For information on dates, visit coloradostatefair.com)

Even before statehood, there was a sense of belonging among the miners, ranchers and railroad people who settled in the shadow of the mountains. The state evolved along the line between Spain's empire and the emerging United States, and was created by politicians (rather than cartographers) who drew straight lines that didn't coincide with any natural barriers. It was a geometric shape imposed on a fluid concoction of Native, Spanish and American cultures.

Yet from the first days of Denver there was a palpable identity, a feeling that the territory would become something greater than its elements. From the opening of the Santa Fe Trail in the 1830s and the subsequent gold rushes, the evolution happened rapidly and with purpose. The first cabin was built in Denver in 1858, and just six years later there was an Enabling Act for statehood (1864). Despite the fact that President Andrew Johnson vetoed the Act of Admission twice, in 1866 and 1867, Colorado was admitted to the Union as the 38th state on August 1st, 1876, less than twenty years after the first gold rush. The speed of the transition speaks of determination and purpose, a collective identity and a shared vision.

On November 5, 1872, Ulysses Grant defeated Horace Greeley in a landslide victory for his second term (286 to 66 electoral college votes). Twenty-four days later, Greeley died. Grant's first term began in March 1869, but a few months prior to that he had visited what was then the Territory of Colorado. As the Republican nominee for President, he explored Golden along with William Tecumseh Sherman and Phil Sheridan. The trip was a quick getaway from the campaign trail, and served no real political purpose except to recharge his batteries.

President Ulysses Simpson Grant, with his wife Julia and son Jesse, at their seaside cottage in Long Beach, N.J., which was demolished in 1963. (G.W. Pach, 1872)

He returned to the city just after his second inaugural, in April of 1873. He also visited Black Hawk, traveling along track that his son had helped lay two years earlier, and he stayed at the brand new Teller House hotel in Central City that had been completed in 1872. That edifice was the centerpiece of the community, and was often described as the finest hotel west of the Mississippi. Its builder, Henry Teller (see previous chapter), was an old friend of Grant's.

Sometimes the new communities rallied around something less positive than a Presidential visit. One terrible tale came out of the mountains just after Grant's second visit. Late that fall, a group of about twenty prospectors left Utah for the San Juans, and arrived in the camp of the Ute Chief Ouray at the beginning of January, 1874. The Natives advised strongly against going farther into the mountains at that time of year, and most of the party listened. But there was gold fever in the veins of five of the men. Led by Alfred Packer, who suffered from epilepsy and had failed Cavalry medicals a number of times, they set out that February for the Los Piños agency in the Cochetopa Hills near Gunnison. There was no word from them again until April, when Packer arrived alone at Los Piños.

The tale that eventually emerged was horrific. As members of the party succumbed to cold and hunger, the others ate them. When it got down to the last two, they fought. Packer won.

Packer was jailed and, while the Hinsdale County coroner and a party of witnesses were examining the bodies (which had been discovered by a Harper's Weekly artist the following August), he escaped from the simple log and stacked stone jailhouse in Saguache. He went on the run for most of the next decade and was discovered in a saloon in Fort Fetterman, just north of Douglas, Wyoming. He was arrested, and the image at right is probably an official prison image from this incarceration. He was extradited to Lake City, Colorado, for a trial that took place in April, 1883. Found guilty, he was sentenced to hang. But the sentence was overturned because the events had taken place when Colorado was a Territory, and at the time there was no murder statute. Two years later, he was retried in Gunnison and convicted on five counts of manslaughter. He was paroled in 1901 and worked as a guard at the Denver Post for a while. He died in 1907.

Alfred Packer, who ate parts of five fellow prospectors he may have murdered in the San Juan Mountains during the winter of 1874.

In October of 1875 a Constitutional Convention was convened in Denver to draft a new state Constitution. The draft was adopted the following spring, the male white voters approved it in a ballot in July, and on August 1st 1876, President Grant signed the proclamation admitting Colorado to the Union as the 38th state. Because this occurred one hundred years after the Declaration of independence, Colorado is nicknamed the Centennial State.

This page from Frank Leslie's illustrated newspaper, vol. 51 depicts the anti-Chinese riot that took place in Denver on October 31st, 1880.

The previous year, Grant had signed another less enlightened proclamation, the racially driven Page Act. It was the first piece of U.S. legislation to restrict immigration, and it specifically targeted anybody from Asia who had been brought to these shores to be a forced laborer, and any Asian woman who would engage in prostitution. How an immigration official was to determine these qualifications was not very specific.

The Act's sponsor was Horace F. Page, a California lawyer and Republican whose intent was to curb the availability of cheap Chinese labor, and also the growth of Chinese brothels in his state. The ban on Asian women immigrating was especially well enforced, and created great hardship in part because it split up families. Colorado was not immune from anti-Chinese action. The year before the Page Act, miners at Nederland forcefully evicted one hundred and sixty Chinese people from the camp. The settlement, located seventeen miles southwest of Boulder, was known as Brown's Crossing until 1871, and then became Nederland in 1874 when the Caribou Mine was sold to the Nederland Mining Company from Holland.

In 1880 there were a little over two hundred Chinese nationals living in Denver. During the presidential election that fall, the Democratic candidate, Winfield Hancock, came out in favor of a ban on Chinese immigration. Then the

Democrat-leaning Rocky Mountain News published a campaign attacking Chinese values and effects on the community. Incensed, a 3,000-strong mob led by Irish laborers attacked the city's small Chinatown in the afternoon of October 31st, destroying homes and burning businesses, and beating anyone they caught. One man, a laundry worker named Sing Lee, was beaten to death in the street.

The mayor ordered the fire department to hose down the mob, which only incited them to greater depravities. Many residents heroically sheltered Chinese people, including a gambler who pulled his pistol and ran off a group of rioters bent on burning a laundry, and the madam of a brothel whose girls armed themselves to save dozens of potential victims. Eventually the police rounded up the Chinese people and locked them in jail for their own safety. Nobody was prosecuted, no reparations were made for the looted and burned homes and businesses, and Sing Lee's murderers were acquitted the following year.

Denver's Chinatown survived until World War II, when it was demolished to make way for urban development. Today, approximately 3.7% of the city's population is Asian. Denver's overall

demographics have changed significantly since the race riot of 1880. Today, more than 30% of the population is Hispanic/Latino, and many other races are well represented. While no city is perfect, Denver today is recognized nationally as a very progressive, inclusive community that celebrates its diversity and builds opportunities for all of its citizens.

Exploration

Between 1870 and 1879 a series of expedition were led by Lieutenant George Wheeler who was charged with exploring west of the 100th Meridian that runs down through the centers of what are now Nebraska and Kansas. His task was to map the country at a scale of 8 miles to the inch At left is an image made by the expedition's official photographer, Timothy O'Sullivan, showing the start of one stage of the adventure, as Mohave Indians joined the party as guides on the Colorado River. The party created hundreds of high-resolution photographic images, including the 1874 O'Sullivan shot below. It shows "Beaver Lake at 9000 feet above sea level twenty miles from the mouth of Conejos Cañon". Note how the lone (unidentified) figure standing on the near shoreline lends the image scale and perspective.

Located high in the La Garita Mountain Range in Southern Colorado, there is a 640-acre Geologic Area named after George Wheeler. The park sits in the Rio Grande National Forest, near the town of Creede, and its rock formations are simply astounding.

Other photographers also recorded the wilderness, as exploratory parties ventured far beyond the bounds of common sense. In 1873, William Henry Jackson made the image below somewhere in the Colorado Rocky Mountains. Taken for the Detroit Publishing Company, he titled it "The Photographer's Assistants". Jackson, a New York native, was a talented painter who saw action as a nineteen-year-old at Gettysburg. After the war, he and his brother Edward moved to Nebraska, where William began to explore the potential of photography. In 1869, he was hired as a Union Pacific photographer, and the next year became part of what would become the U.S. Geographical Survey.

At right is a somewhat indistinct shot taken in front of a150 foot tall rock in Pleasant Park. It is now part of a beautifully landscaped golf course called Perry Park Golf and Country Club that's located in southwestern Douglas County, about forty minute's drive south of Denver. Constant Duhem made this image in 1874, and it shows his brother Victor in the foreground with the photographers' wagon. Together, they operated the Duhem Brothers Photography Studio, which was located at 448 Larimer St. in Denver. They created a number of stereo-views of natural features throughout the state, helping to form the nucleus of what would become one of Colorado's greatest economic strengths, the tourism industry.

Stereo-views, or stereographs, were two slightly different versions of the same photograph placed side-by-side on a cardboard backer, and then looked at simultaneously through a viewer called a stereoscope. The pictures were taken from two spots a few inches or feet apart. The effect was to deliver the perception/illusion of a three-dimensional image that has focal depth. The brain translated the pair of two-dimensional pictures into a single three-dimensional one.

On the next page is another image from a stereo-view, this time made by photographer B.A. Hawkins in 1875. It shows men and a wagon posed in front of shop on 16th Street in Denver. On the wagon it says: "Home from the Black Hills, busted". The store is called Colorado Curiosities, and it was most likely a taxidermist's shop. There's a stuffed elk with a huge rack behind the wagon, and a buffalo hide hanging from the wall to the right of the elk, between the windows. There's a man standing in the doorway dressed in a white shirt and straw hat, whom one might assume is the store's proprietor. To his left are wolf skins and to his right is a mounted bear's head. Plus, there are coyote pelts on the front of the wagon, draped over the shafts.

The temptation to photograph Colorado's virtually endless vistas was just too much for most mortal men. As more and more of the state opened up to travel, people began to make special trips just to see what Mother Nature had created in their backyard. Others took in the views as they

traveled through the mountains for work. At left is an image by Eugene Brandt, made in 1876. It shows the U.S. Signal Station that was built in 1873 atop Pike's Peak. The stone section was 18 x 30 feet. Note the man on the roof, installing or perhaps adjusting an anemometer (an instrument used to measure and record wind speed).

At right is a William Gunnison Chamberlain photograph from 1878 showing an unidentified man standing atop a large rock, aiming a gun. The photographer noted the location as Monument Park, which presumably is the area near Grand Junction that was preserved in 1911 as Colorado National Monument, and now in the care of the National Park Service. There, amid spectacular rock formations, Monument Canyon weaves through the desert amid forests of pinyon pine and juniper.

New Institutions

On November 1st, 1876, the new Colorado bicameral (two houses) legislature met for the first time in Denver. That initial session ran until March 20, 1877. One of the legislature's earliest concerns was education, and in 1877 the University of Colorado opened on the Boulder campus. Today, it is one of just thirty-four public institutions belonging to the prestigious Association of American Universities (AAU). In 1879, the Colorado Historical Society was formed. Today, History Colorado is a 501(c)(3) charitable organization and an agency of the State of Colorado under the Department of Higher Education (online at historycolorado.org). The assembly met every other year until World War II, and in 1950 it began to meet every year. There are one hundred representatives: the House has sixty-five members and the Senate has thirty-five. House members are elected to two-year terms, and in the Senate the term is four years.

Senator Horace Tabor
(Brady-Handy, 1875)

After education, the next piece of infrastructure that a growing state needs is communication technology. Today's Qwest Corporation began life in 1879 as the Denver Telephone Dispatch Company, which opened for business on February 24th. It was founded by Frederick Vaille, Henry Walcott and Sam Morgan, was a franchise of the Bell Telephone Company, and started life with just 161 customers. Western Union became a direct competitor by way of its Colorado Edison Telephone Company, but it was soon absorbed by Bell. By the late 1880s Bell was king in Colorado and remained so for the next one hundred and ten years. In a very short space of time, Colorado had gone from wilderness to railroads, cities and state-of-the-art technology.

One microcosm of the transition from rough mining colonies to statehood was the life of Horace Austin Warner Tabor. Born in Vermont in 1830, Tabor became a stonemason and very early in his adult life, he adopted strong anti-slavery views. In an effort to keep slavery out of Kansas so that the Territory would enter the Union as a free state, he moved there in 1855 as part of the New England Emigrant Aid Company. That was a Boston-based organization designed to transport abolitionists out west and change the composition of the electorate.

Tabor's second wife, the once glamorous Elizabeth "Baby Doe", is shown here in a full-length portrait that superimposed her photograph on a pencil drawing of the entrance to the Matchless Silver Mine in Leadville. She lived there in a shack, in poverty, from the time of her husband's death in 1899 until her own demise in 1935. (Jewel Popkin, 1934)

In 1859, newly married and looking for financial security, he and his wife Augusta moved to Leadville after a couple of brief stops in other mining settlements. The next year the couple moved to Buckskin Joe, near Alma, where they set up in the mercantile business. Their store prospered over the next few years, and the Tabors began to invest in mines. Horace also prospected, but by 1868 the placer gold was running thin and the Tabors relocated to Leadville where they set up the store and incorporated the Post Office within it. In January 1878, Horace was elected Mayor.

That May, silver was discovered in the Little Pittsburg mine, and as luck would have it, Tabor had grubstaked the prospectors. He owned one third of the yield, and was on his way to riches. A millionaire, he started a newspaper and bank, and even built an opera house in Leadville, and eventually another in Denver. And Tabor's political career followed the same trajectory as his businesses. He was elected Lieutenant Governor of the state, and even served as a U.S. Senator for ninety days when Henry Teller resigned before the end of his term to serve as U.S. Secretary of the Interior. And then things began to slow down. Tabor divorced Augusta and married Elizabeth 'Baby Doe' McCourt, causing a bit of a scandal. He ran for Governor four times but never won, and in 1893 when Grover Cleveland repealed the Sherman Silver Purchase Act (a bill that required the government to purchase large amounts of the metal for coinage and also for currency manipulation), his fortune diminished substantially. He got a job as the postmaster in Denver, but died within a year, of appendicitis. Augusta, however, survived the financial woes and became one of the wealthiest inhabitants of Denver.

It took a lot of personal courage for men such as Horace Tabor to prospect in the vastness of South Park.

One can feel some sense of the challenge when looking at this photograph of six men in front of the Dolly Varden Mine, located on Mount Bross with Mt. Lincoln in the background. William Gunnison Chamberlain made this picture in 1878. The ore was located in 1872 by George W. Brunk and Assyria Hall, and the mine eventually produced more than a million dollars worth of silver. In 1881, an explosion in one of the shafts killed 24-year-old James Parks, a married miner originally from Pennsylvania, who was attempting to reignite a fuse on some dynamite.

Mud flowing, snowmelt and flash floods in spring were just a few of the dangers associated with hydraulic mining – using water under pressure to dislodge rocks, gravel and topsoil. In placer mining, the slurry is channeled through sluice boxes to remove the gold. This 1878 image by William Gunnison Chamberlain records hydraulic mining in the California Gulch, near Leadville.

By 1999, the last of the lead, gold, silver, copper, zinc, and manganese deposits in the eighteen square mile California Gulch site had been exhausted. Beginning in 1983 with studies, and in 1995 with hands-on involvement, a combination of the Environmental Protection Agency (EPA), the state of Colorado, several local communities and some mining companies began working on cleaning up what has been declared a Superfund Site. Both the soil and the Arkansas River were contaminated with heavy metals. According to the EPA, "Wastes generated during the mining and ore processing activities contained metals such as arsenic and lead at levels posing a threat to human health and the environment. These wastes remained on the land surface and migrated through the environment by washing into streams and leaching contaminants into surface water and groundwater." There has been substantial progress and in late 2014, the EPA website noted that "Most of the cleanup at this site has been completed, so current risk of exposure is low". For the latest progress, visit www2.epa.gov/region8/california-gulch.

In 1869, President Grant appointed Edward McCook Governor of the Territory of Colorado. During his tenure McCook, a former Union general and a supporter of women's suffrage, signed the legislation that would eventually create Colorado State University. (M. Brady, c.1863)

When prospectors such as Horace Tabor struck a rich mineral vein, the camps and settlements and towns they created often lived and died with the quality, quantity and accessibility of the ore. Some towns survived longer than the strike because they diversified their economies with mills and merchants, or perhaps a railroad came through. Cities such as Pueblo, Denver, Fort Collins, Colorado Springs and Grand Junction embraced diversity in areas such as the arts, medicine and education. As their populations increased, intellectual opportunities expanded.

In 1879, there was a significant leap forward for education. In 1870, Governor Edward McCook had signed a bill establishing an agricultural college at Fort Collins, but for nine long years it remained unfunded, then underfunded. It wasn't until 1874 that the first bricks were laid for a building about the size of a single car garage. On July 27th 1878, two years after statehood, the cornerstone for the first major building, Old Main was laid. The Agricultural College of Colorado opened its doors to students in 1879, with President Elijah Edwards and two faculty members on staff. The school became the Colorado State College of Agriculture and

Mechanic Arts, or Colorado A&M in 1935, and on May 1st 1957, the Colorado General Assembly approved the new name of Colorado State University. The 1907 photograph below from the National Archives shows thirty-one forestry students on the campus of the Colorado Agricultural College in Fort Collins.

By 2014, Colorado State University had almost 27,000 undergraduate students enrolled. The University is a Carnegie Class I research institution and has approximately 1,550 faculty in eight colleges and 55 academic departments. To date, there are more than 170,000 living alumni, and the university had contributed immensely to the development and growth of the state, and to the lives, welfare and quality of life of its population.

Chapter 6
Building Communities

The evolution from Territory to State was especially evident in the way people built. Shacks and cabins very quickly gave way to brick, stone, millwork and leaded glass. Immigrants tend to contribute what they know to a new culture, and Colorado's early architecture was as diverse as its people. One of the best surviving edifices in the state is the Granite Building at 15th and Larimer in downtown Denver, shown **below** in a c.1969 view by HABS.

The structure was built for the McNamara Dry Goods Co. and was originally known as the Graham-Clayton Building after the partnership that erected it in 1882. There is strong evidence that the site it occupies was once the location of the first cabin built by William Larimer and his son, who were among the founders of Denver. By the end of the Depression the building was beginning to see hard times, and during the 1950s it became a flophouse. Its revival began in the early 1960s with the courage and determination of preservationists such as the Larimer Square Associates, who were led by Dana Crawford. The oldest survivor of Denver's imposing Victorian grand structures, the Granite owes its current resurrection to the vision of businessman Jeff Hermanson, who purchased the property in 1993. In large part because of his efforts, the Granite building is now an essential element in a vibrant shopping, restaurant and entertainment complex, Larimer Square (larimersquare.com), which is on the National Register of Historic Places.

Great architecture was not limited to Denver, and is by no means defined by scale. For example, Crested Butte is a town of about 1,500 souls located 100 miles east of Grand Junction as the crow flies (152 by road). Howard Smith, who built a smelter and sawmill there, laid out the streets in 1878. The town was incorporated in 1880, and the Denver & Rio Grande arrived the following November. The Town Hall (shown **above** in a 1978 HABS photograph by Walter Smalling) was built in 1883 and served in that capacity until 1952. According to the Gunnison-Crested Butte website, "it was designed and built in an eastern European manner by Jacob

Kochevar. This beautiful building did double duty for the Trustees [city council members] and the Fire Department, with its second floor hall being used for dances, church, and public meetings. Portions of the building were once inadvertently blown up when the town tried to stop a raging fire that was destroying Elk Avenue. Dynamite charges were set in the street to halt the fire's advance and ended up blowing up windows on surrounding blocks. For a period of time, the UCLA Pasadena theater brought students for a two month long season of melodrama. In 1991, the town temporarily moved the building into the middle of Second Street and rebuilt the crumbling foundation." (gunnisoncrestedbutte.com)

Municipal buildings are usually a reflection of the size and wealth of the population, and by the 1880 census Colorado was already home to just under two hundred thousand citizens (about four times what it had been a decade earlier). One of them was George Schleier, who between 1864 and 1884 was a real estate developer in Denver. Prior to that, he had been one of the first settlers in the

area, and built the first two-story home. In the early 1880s he contracted with architect E.F. Edbrooke to build a new home at what is now 1665 Grant Street. The structure was completed around 1888 and features an unusual detail, an onion-shaped dome atop a round tower. The house (**at left** in a c.1981 HABS image) was executed in local red sandstone and is eclectic in nature, not conforming to any particular architectural style, and with elements of Tudor, Queen Anne and Victorian influence. Within, the millwork is complex, incorporating turned and carved elements with extensive wainscoting and raised panel work (see detail, **below**: HABS c.1981). There are eight elaborate fireplaces, many of which include tile and metalwork, and the home boasts some exquisite plasterwork. It is currently being renovated.

Note the large, out-of-place fluorescent ceiling fixture above the stairwell. The Public Service Company of Colorado was founded in 1869. That was the year William Byers (publisher of the

Rocky Mountain News) and seven other businessmen decided to finance a local gas lighting utility called Denver Gas Company. In 1881, Walter Cheesman founded the Colorado Electric Company to capitalize on the recent invention of the arc lamp. Four years later, that company was awarded the city's street lighting contract. In 1889 a number of smaller electricity suppliers merged with Colorado Electric and became the Denver Consolidated Electric Company. In 1891, Denver Gas followed suit, merging with its competitors and became Denver Consolidated Gas Company. After the bottom fell out of the silver market in 1893, and a recession ensued, the two organizations merged as Denver Gas & Electric Company (DG&E). After more mergers and acquisitions, the entire conglomeration was incorporated under the PSCo name on September 3rd 1924. By World War II it was providing 80% of Colorado's gas and electricity needs.

The Union Depot and Railroad Co. opened Denver's Union Station on June 1st 1881 (above, in a 1908 Detroit Publishing Co. image). Before then, separate railroads had their own depots. It burned in March of 1884, and was quickly rebuilt with a lower roofline and a stone clock tower. In 1906, the Welcome Arch had been added (next page, in a 1910 photograph by Underwood & Underwood). In 1914 the clock tower was demolished and the center section was expanded to the current profile (at right).

After Union Station opened that summer (1881), the voters of Colorado officially made Denver their state capital in November. The city was starting to take on the air of a cosmopolitan center.

Horace Tabor had built the Grand Opera House, which opened that year (**left**). Unfortunately, it was torn down in 1964, but on its debut it was considered one of the most opulent and extravagant buildings between the Mississippi and San Francisco. The theatre occupied an entire block at 16th and Curtis, currently home to a branch of the Federal Reserve Bank. The Granite Building followed in 1882, and the magnificent Brown Palace Hotel was built a decade later, in 1892. (History buffs can book a tour of the latter at brownpalace.com.) Shown **below** is the Dining Room at the Brown Palace, in a C.H. Graves photograph from 1900. Another building of note was the Croke Patterson Campbell mansion at 11th and Pennsylvania (**lower left**).

Built in 1890 of local sandstone, it took the form of a French chateau. Thomas Croke was a merchant and politician, and in 1892 he sold the property to Thomas Patterson, a U.S. Congressman and later Senator, who published the Rocky Mountain News until 1913. His son-in-law, Richard C. Campbell, was a Denver businessman, state senator, and also had an interest in the News. The home has been

through various uses over the years, which included periods as both apartments and offices. In 2013 it was offered for sale (the agent claimed it was haunted). The most impressive building in the state, the Colorado State Capitol Building, wasn't erected until 1894.

To crown the metropolitan atmosphere of the new capital, Colorado played host to one of the world's most cosmopolitan figures in 1882. Oscar Wilde visited Denver on a lecture tour, and he also spent time in Leadville, where he went down the Matchless Mine and enjoyed what he described as a five-course meal with the miners.

"The first course was whiskey," he said. "The second course was whiskey…"

Wilde (**at right**, in a Napoleon Sarony portrait published the year he visited Denver) was born in Dublin, Ireland in 1854 and would eventually become the most celebrated playwright in London. A student of the Arts & Crafts movement philosopher John Ruskin, he spent some time in the United States and Canada lecturing on English Renaissance in Art. Wilde later penned works such as his only novel *The Picture of Dorian Gray*, and the stage masterpiece *The Importance of Being Earnest*. In 1897 he was convicted of homosexuality and imprisoned for two years hard labor. Upon his release he moved to Paris where he died, penniless, the next year (1900), at the age of 46.

The year that Wilde visited Colorado, there was a strong earthquake along the northern Front Range. It was also the year that the federal Chinese Exclusion Act was passed and signed into law by Chester Arthur. A more stringent version of the earlier Page Act, it included an absolute 10-year moratorium on both skilled and unskilled Chinese laborers and especially those employed in mining. It essentially made it impossible for any Chinese national living in the U.S. to re-enter the country if they crossed a border. Congress also used the Act to prohibit both state and federal courts from granting American citizenship to Chinese resident aliens, although these courts could still deport them. Through this and the subsequent Geary Act (which required each Chinese resident to register and obtain a certificate of residence) and several other rulings, the U.S. had specifically anti-Chinese immigration statutes in effect until, essentially, the passing of the Immigration Act of 1965.

More than ten thousand Chinese laborers worked on the Central Pacific alone, and thousands more blasted through the mountains and laid track year-round, with an incredibly high fatality rate. When the railroad work petered out, many Chinese settlers opened laundries, dry goods stores and even opium dens in the towns that had sprung up along the rails. Denver's Chinatown was centered around 20th and Market, and was home to more than a thousand people at its peak.

In 1887, the Colorado Midland started service between Leadville and Colorado City. The line ran through Buena Vista, where it traversed the Hop Gulch on a high trestle (**below**, 1890 by William Henry Jackson), and it was the first Colorado standard gauge line to cross the Continental Divide (via the Hagerman Tunnel). It arrived in Aspen just after the D&RG.

Buena Vista was home for a while to one of the region's most celebrated photographers, John Grabill. He was born in 1849 in Donnelsville, Ohio, and by 1881 he had moved to Colorado. On his travels, he had gained a background in both mining and railroad photography. Those areas of expertise may have served him well in Buena Vista, which was incorporated in 1879 and catered to silver, gold and lead mines. Both the Denver & Rio Grande and the South Park & Pacific served the surrounding area. The year after Grabill left (1886), the Colorado Midland arrived in Buena Vista. In 1881, Grabill is mentioned as a partner of noted miner Nelson D. Wanamaker, who had discovered gem aquamarines on Mount Antero in Chaffee County.

Wanamaker also found tungsten ore in Boulder County. In keeping with that occupation, an 1882 map of Buena Vista shows Grabill as operating a mining exchange office in the town (see photo **below**, by Grabill dated 1888 but probably taken in 1886), from which we may gather that he speculated in metals. But his real passion was photography, for which he had an innate talent that is evinced by a number of plates that survive, and their superior composition and lighting.

Above is the photographic studio of John Grabill in Buena Vista, and in the foreground is his Mining Exchange.

In 1886, Grabill left Colorado and opened a photographic studio in Sturgis, a couple of miles from Fort Meade in Dakota Territory. This was the site of an Army fort used by the US Cavalry to patrol a large area of the Black Hills, some of the Powder River basin, and the plains to the north and east of the Hills. He took many photographs of soldiers in training at the fort, and also posed portraits of officers and other notables who passed through, many of whom were Native American. Because of his connections at the post, he had the ignoble honor of photographing scenes after the massacre at Wounded Knee in 1890.

In October 1887, a small encampment of soldiers eight miles southwest of Denver was the first step in the construction of another military installation, Fort Logan, which was eventually completed in 1897. It remained in use until 1946 when part of it then became a National Cemetery. The site was selected by Phil Sheridan and donated by Denver businessmen.

The fort was home to the 7th Infantry and some Cavalry units. In 1894, troops from Fort Logan were dispatched to Denver to put down a riot. Governor Davis Hanson Waite had fired the police and fire commissioners in an effort to curtail corruption, but the officials refused to evacuate the offices at City Hall. Others who were in fear of their jobs soon joined them, and after they erected barricades the Governor called in the troops. The Supreme Court ruled in his favor, saying he had the right to remove the commissioners, but in the wake of the City Hall War, Waite lost the next election.

On 18th December, 1888, rancher Richard Wetherill and his brother-in-law Charlie Mason were looking for strays in canyons near their ranch in the southwest corner of the state. Wetherill had heard from Ute neighbors that there were some homes of ancient people in one particular canyon, but he had ranched there since 1881 and never came across them. On this day, the men looked down through a snowstorm from a mesa, and gazed upon the 700-year-old Cliff Palace at Mesa Verde. It became a National Park in 1906.

In June 1889, librarian John Cotton Dana established the Denver Public Library in the city's high school. It wasn't until 1910 that the Library moved into a building of its own, which was paid for by Andrew Carnegie.

*Above: Andrew Carnegie in 1913 by Marceau Studio, New York. **At right**, the new Central Library in Denver.*

Over the next decade, Carnegie built eight branch libraries throughout the city. Born in Scotland, he was one of America's most successful entrepreneurs and was at the forefront of a massive expansion of the steel industry in the latter part of the nineteenth century. By his death in 1919, he had given about 90% of his vast fortune (today, about $5 billion) to philanthropic causes, especially local libraries. In that same spirit the people of Denver overwhelmingly voted to build an extraordinary architectural masterpiece, the 540,000 square-foot Central Library. Designed

by Michael Graves and the firm of Klipp Colussy Jenks DuBois, it opened in 1995. Libraries across Colorado have always been held in high regard, and even small communities pay tribute to learning by housing their collections well. In September 1940, for example, Russell Lee photographed the Walsh Library in Ouray for the Farm Security Administration (**at left**). It occupied part of the brick City Hall building that had been erected in 1900. The structure was also home to the Fire Department. It was designed as a smaller replica of Independence Hall in Philadelphia, and was constructed with funds donated by Thomas Walsh, who discovered and worked the Camp Bird Mine. The library occupies the second floor, and bears Walsh's name. The structure burned in January 1950, and was restored in 1988. The library is still upstairs.

While Denver continued to grow at a tremendous rate through the 1870s and early 1880s, the population around the rest of the state often shifted with the fortunes of silver mines, and the encroachment of new railroads. The census of 1890 determined that the population of Colorado was over 413,249. It would have been at least five more had it not been for an unsavory incident that culminated near the new state prison in Cañon City late in 1888. The story began with a drifter named George Witherell, who had been convicted back in 1871 of murdering a man named Wahl.

He had first shot his victim and then dragged him to a ravine and hacked the body to pieces with an axe. He then took Mr. Wahl's wagon and mule team and sold them. Nine years into his sentence, Governor Alva Adams was presented with an appeal and, as there were no witnesses to the crime, he granted a pardon and released Witherell in April, 1881. There is some evidence that upon gaining his

freedom, he murdered a woman named Hand and her grandson, but he was never charged and the bodies were never discovered.

Mr. Witherell disappeared from sight for a while and didn't resurface until 1888, when he turned up in the employ (or possibly a business partner) of a young man named Charles McCain who was in the moving and hauling business in Pueblo. The two drove a pair of McCain's wagons to Beaver Creek to move a household, and a couple of days later McCain's wife received a letter, purportedly from her husband, saying that he had sold the stock and was leaving her. She immediately contacted the law and a posse found Witherell in Denver, trying to sell McCain's wagons. Two days later, they discovered his body, shot and hacked with an axe, and left in a ravine near Turkey Creek.

Two months later, Witherell was extradited from Denver to Cañon City, but when the sheriff arrived with his prisoner a group of citizens knocked on the jailhouse door and asked him to hand over the murderer. Witherell was taken from the county jail to a telephone pole on 1st and Main, where a wire was put around his neck and he was hung (**at left**, unattributed). Nobody was ever charged in the incident.

Not everything was so serious in the early days of the state. In an excellent article on historynet.com, author Gregory Lalire gives a stirring account of the origins of 'Baseball in the West". According to the piece, "students at Colorado College in Colorado Springs organized a baseball team in 1880. The Colorado State League formed in 1885, with teams in Colorado Springs, Leadville, Pueblo and Denver. The next year the Denver Mountain Lions won the Western League title with a 54–26 record. Other Denver minor league teams through the years have included the Mountaineers, Grizzlies, Solis, Gulfs, Zephyrs and Bears. The Mile-High City finally landed in the majors with the Rockies in 1993." [historynet.com/baseball-in-the-west-2.htm]

Two baseball cards issued in 1888 by the tobacco company Goodwin & Co. show pitcher Ed Silch and team manager Rowe. The team is not mentioned, other than the 'Denvers', but may have been the Denver Mountain Lions of the Colorado State League.

Beyond sports, other cultural organizations had an early start in the state. The American Turners was founded in Cincinnati, Ohio in 1848 by German immigrants, and opened a branch in Denver in 1865. In June 1913, the national organization held its annual celebration, the 31st Bundesturnfest, in Colorado. Public buildings throughout the state, from rail depots to stores and hotels were decorated with American and German bunting. The Turner's Hall in east Denver (**below**) was the headquarters of the event. The Turnvereine helped German immigrants assimilate into American society. They were strong supporters of Abraham Lincoln, providing the bodyguard at his inauguration and an honor guard at his funeral. Four years after the Colorado celebration, during World War I, German heritage was not as welcome in America and the German language was banned in schools all across the country. The Turner societies survived that and a similar situation during the second war, and by 1948 the Post Office issued a 3-cent commemorative stamp marking the 100th anniversary of the movement in the United States. Today, about fifty Turner societies still exist, with headquarters in Louisville, Kentucky. The Turner Hall burned in July 1920 and the Turnverein moved to 1570 Clarkson Street in 1922. Today, it is primarily a non-profit dance organization.

On July 4th 1890, the cornerstone was placed for the erection of a new State Capitol on a small mound called Brown's Bluff in downtown Denver. Erected in white Colorado granite, it was designed to imitate the national Capitol building in Washington. The Colorado building (at right, in a 1906 C.L. Wasson photograph taken for International Stereograph Co.) has a dome that was plated in 24-karat gold in 1908, which was done to symbolize the state's rich mineral resources and the gold rushes that brought European settlement. Here is how Denver's online business and tourism guide, milehighcity.com, described the interior in 2014:

"Inside is a cacophony of brilliant brass and stained glass. The dome towers 180 feet above, and contains stained glass dedicated to the 16 initial founders of the city of Denver. The interior of the capitol was built with the rare and priceless Colorado Rose Onyx or what is commonly called Beulah Red Marble, named after the city in which it was found. The rose marble was quarried at Yule Creek in Gunnison County at the foothills of the Greenhorn Mountains. The mauve marble is so rare that its known supply was completely used up in the process of beautifying the capitol. The cutting, polishing, and installing of the marble took six years, from 1894 to 1900. Also inside you'll find hand painted originals of each of the U.S. presidents, from George Washington to Bill Clinton. There are three main rooms where the actual legislating takes place, the House Gallery, the Senate Gallery, and the House of Representatives."

The same year Wasson made the image above, E.W. Kelley of the Universal View Co. published the photograph **below**. It's a view looking up 16ᵗʰ Street toward the new Capitol. A tram is approaching on the right-hand tracks, there are farmers with hay wagons to the right of them, and there's an impressive array of insulators atop the telegraph poles at left (72 on each).

The year that Denver laid the state Capitol cornerstone (1890), a lot was happening in and around Colorado Springs. That October, a ranch hand/prospector named Bob Womack discovered some placer gold and then veins in the bed of Cripple Creek, on the southwest face of Pike's Peak. Over the next decade, the rush would result in more than 500 paying claims, and the birth of two towns – Cripple Creek and Victor. The bond in which the gold was held required chlorination and cyanide leaching, rather than a simple stamp mill. Among the mines were the C.O.D., the Independence, the Vindicator and the Portland, and combined this field produced more gold than any other in Colorado. (**Below**: *1899 photograph of a Pike's Peak prospector, by William Henry Jackson.*)

The same month Bob Womack struck gold, the Manitou & Pike's Peak completed a rack-and-pinion line to the top of Pike's Peak (**below**, William Henry Jackson, 1900). On the next page is another Jackson image from the same visit, showing the station and hotel at the summit.

The following year, the Broadmoor Hotel and its casino (**below**) opened near Colorado Springs. It was the brainchild of a Prussian immigrant, Count James Pourtales, whose first local investment was a dairy farm that he purchased from William Wilcox. The hotel sits on manmade Cheyenne Lake, and was designed by architect Lindley Johnson. It succumbed to fire in 1897, and a new casino was opened the following year. Spencer Penrose purchased the property in 1916.

Today, the Broadmoor (**at right**, c1918) still welcomes guests to Colorado Springs with impeccable service and distinctive amenities. It operates the only Five-Star, Five-Diamond restaurant in Colorado, along with 54 holes of championship golf, six tennis courts, indoor and outdoor pools and distinctive retail shops. It also has 185,000 square feet of meeting space.

In 1879, silver strikes along the Roaring Fork River caused an influx of miners and the businesses that support them. That year, Henry Gillespie laid out the streets of a town he named Ute City, which

was renamed Aspen the following year. **At left**, in an 1890 image by the Kilburn Brothers, a man leads a pack mule carrying two children along a steep trail, with Aspen in the background.

Below is an 1892 unattributed image of the San Juan & New York Mining & Smelting Company in Durango. The original print belongs to the Strater Hotel. The photograph was made just two years after the Denver and Rio Grande created the city on the banks of the Animas River

where Ute travelers had camped for centuries, and there is evidence of Pueblo settlement dating to the eighth century. Through somewhat questionable means, the railroad purchased the site, which was ideal for the location of a smelter. It was relatively accessible, had an abundant water supply, and coal was available locally. The name was Spanish in origin: there is a Durango in Spain, and another in Mexico.

The nearby establishment of two major tourism attractions, the San Juan National Forest (1905) and Mesa Verde National Park (1906), along with breathtaking scenery and a hospitable populace, turned Durango into a travel destination. Today, the city has a population of about 17,000, an airport and a ski resort (durangomountainresort.com). It is also home to Fort Lewis College, a public, four-year liberal arts campus located on a 247-acre site atop a mesa overlooking the Animas River Valley and downtown Durango. Of particular interest to history buffs is the Durango & Silverton narrow gauge railroad that still travels a spectacular route carved through the mountains more than a century ago.

Above: Arapahoe Basin ski resort (image undated, unattributed, via photostash.org 2014)

San Juan and Mesa Verde were not the first national icons to be set aside and preserved in Colorado. In October of 1891, an executive order by President Benjamin Harrison created the White River Plateau Timberland Reserve, which would become the White River National Forest in 1905. The first reserve in Colorado and second in the nation, it initially included more than 1.1 million acres, and today covers an astounding 2.3 million acres, with ten peaks over 14,000 feet. Known around the world as a skier's paradise, one of the White River's earliest attractions was Hayden Peak near Aspen, where investors built the Highland Bavaria Lodge on Castle Creek at the base of the mountain during the 1930s. In the '40s, Aspen Mountain outshone Hayden Peak because of easier accessibility, and in 1946 two chair lifts were installed in Aspen. Vail and Snowmass became popular in the 1960s. However, Hayden Peak is still a popular backcountry ski destination, with a 4,000-foot descent. Arapahoe Basin alpine ski resort (shown **above**, and also known as A-Basin), began when Max and

Edna Dercum built the Ski Tip Lodge in the 1940s. Located about seventy miles west of Denver near the town of Dillon, the area enjoys 350 inches of snowfall annually.

In December 1892, Battlement Mesa Forest Reserve was established. It eventually became parts of both the White River and Grand Mesa National Forests.

1892 also saw the founding of Denver's *Evening Post* newspaper, created by supporters of the Democratic Party. It went bankrupt the following year when silver prices crashed, but was revived in 1894. In 1895 the name was changed to the *Denver Evening Post*, and in 1901 it became *The Denver Post* (denverpost.com).

In July of 1893 the teacher, poet and Massachusetts native Katharine Lee Bates (1859 - 1929) climbed to the summit of Pike's Peak. On her return, she penned the first of three versions of the anthem, *America The Beautiful*. Bates was the head of the English department at Wellesley College until her retirement in 1925. Her Colorado visit apparently inspired the lines…

For purple mountain majesties
Above the fruited plain.

Colorado was a source of other patriotic gestures, too, such as the naming of three successive ships of the United States Navy. Shown **at left** is the USS Colorado, a three-masted steam screw frigate that was in commission from 1858–1876. The image is noted at the Library of Congress as a Detroit Publishing Company photograph that was published between 1888 and 1900. However, the vessel was broken up for salvage in 1885. She was moored in the Navy Yard in New York from the time she was decommissioned in 1876 until her demise, so it's probable that the photograph was made during those years.

In 1905, the name passed to a Pennsylvania-class armored cruiser, and in 1923 it was bestowed upon a battleship that survived World War II. A fourth vessel bearing the proud name USS Colorado is a Virginia Class submarine that is currently under construction in Groton, Connecticut. That boat (SSN-788) is expected to be commissioned in 2017.

In the late summer of 1895, Denver was seized by a peculiar religious fervor. Francis Schlatter, a native of Alsace on the French-German border, emerged as a spiritual healer who preached no doctrine and sought no reward. He had gained a reputation for treating the sick in Albuquerque's Old Town that July. Below is a photograph by W.A. White of Raton, New Mexico showing a crowd in Denver waiting for the touch of 'The Healer'. That November, he disappeared, and his body was found in Mexico two years later. Foul play was not suspected. Schlatter, whose only arrest was in Arkansas for vagrancy in 1894, appears to have been a genuine, sincere believer in his own mission, and not a con artist.

About this time near the town of Fort Morgan, which lies some fifty miles east of Greeley, extensive irrigation works were taking place. The settlement had originated some thirty years earlier as Camp Wardell, an Army outpost designed to protect travelers on their way to the new mines around Denver.

The civilian town was platted in 1884 by one of Greeley's leading lights, Abner Baker, and it became the seat of Morgan County in 1889. In 1904, Fort Morgan would be the birthplace of Big Band leader Glenn Miller, who died in a plane crash over the English Channel in 1944 while entertaining the troops. Miller, whose signature tune was *Moonlight Serenade*, was an alumnus of the University of Colorado in Boulder. The image **at left**, made by the Fort Morgan Drug Company in the early 1890s, shows "men spread out across the land using teams of horses to dig ditches

for irrigation". The shot **at right**, from a few years later (c.1895), is by Louis Charles McClure and shows an irrigation canal near Fort Morgan. The area receives about 14 inches of rain and 24 inches of snow annually. Once home to roving Pawnee, the flat plain is ideal for the cultivation of grazing (hay) and wheat. North of town are the Pawnee Buttes, which were featured in James Michener's novel *Centennial*.

In 1896, the Daughters of the American Revolution was incorporated by an Act of Congress. Mary Green Montgomery Slocum founded a DAR state society in Colorado in 1895. Today it has 42 chapters statewide and over 3,000 members dedicated to promoting education, historic preservation and patriotism. DAR is one of the largest women's service organizations in the world.

Also in 1896, the mayor of Denver, Tom McMurry, was given a gift of an orphaned black bear cub. Not knowing what to do with the animal, he handed it off to the City Park gardeners who used this one donation to create what is now the Denver Zoo.

At left, a double streetcar crosses a bridge in Denver c.1895. (Unattributed image.) Below is a Jackson-Smith Photo Company panorama of Denver in 1898.

All through the '90s, cattle were a vibrant sector of the Colorado economy, especially with railroads now connecting the state to both coasts and the cities of the Midwest. Below is a photograph of a roundup on the Cimarron, a small river in the west of the state (as opposed to the larger Cimarron River that crosses the southeastern corner of Colorado into Kansas, and then flows to the Arkansas). This Cimarron flows north out of the Uncompahgre National Forest into the Gunnison River, just west of Blue Mesa Reservoir (it's about half an hour's drive east of Montrose). The photograph was made in 1898 by the Detroit Publishing Company.

The Denver and Rio Grande served the town of Cimarron, and one of its narrow gauge trestle bridges, built in 1895, is still located in Cimarron Canyon, near Morrow Point Dam.

These two images from 1898, released by the Detroit Publishing Company, depict life on the range in Colorado. **Above** is "The Grub Pile", showing a chuck wagon with Cookie in the foreground tending to a Dutch oven. In the calf branding shot **at right** the two men look like they are wearing disheveled versions of Cavalry uniforms, suggesting they may possibly have mustered out recently.

Below, this evocative image by Historic American Buildings Survey (HABS) photographer Arnold Thallheimer was made in 1989. It shows corrals on the John Sanders Cross homestead, which was established by former cowboys just after the turn of the century. Located in Pinon Canyon, it lies eleven miles east of U.S. Highway 350 near Model, in Las Animas County (about twenty miles northwest of Trinidad). What's interesting here is the way that materials were used to create the corral fence. In the foreground, split rails were installed horizontally between posts. In the middle, small branches were used vertically in the Mexican tradition of a coyote fence, and then sawn boards were used for the gates. In the background, barbed wire was strung between posts to enclose a pasture. At right, the rocks became part of the boundary. As they always have, farmers and ranchers used what was available in ingenious ways.

About a hundred miles north of the John Sanders Cross homestead, Colorado Springs briefly played host to one of the nation's most brilliant minds. Croatia-born Nikola Tesla (1856-1943) is best remembered for building the first hydro-electric plant at Niagara Falls, creating the first AC motor, and also developing the AC system that is to this day the global standard for power transmission. Tesla graduated from the Technical University of Graz with a degree in math and science, and did post-graduate work in philosophy at the University of Prague.

Tesla had once worked for Thomas Edison (1884-5), and eventually the two became great rivals. He was also a friend of the writer Mark Twain (whose birth name was Samuel Langhorne Clemens). In a two-year period from 1887 to 1888, he was granted more than thirty patents. In the early 1890s, he demonstrated shortwave radio two years before Marconi, and after his death several of Marconi's patents were reversed in favor of Tesla.

In 1895, there was a devastating fire at Tesla's New York lab. Decades of notes and experimental data were lost. The year before the fire, Tesla had photographed Twain in his New York laboratory, using phosphorous as a lighting agent.

In 1898, Tesla moved to Colorado Springs for two years. He set up a small laboratory, which was operational for seven months before he returned to New York in 1900. There, backed by J.P.Morgan, he began working on what would eventually become a failed effort to create the world's first global communications system. He died in relative poverty and obscurity in a hotel in New York in 1943, suffering from a long-term, mild mental illness.

Nicola Tesla in a Bain News Service portrait, c.1886.

Mining was also doing will at the end of the century. The top image **below** is a Detroit Photographic Co. photograph titled 'Dugout Cabins', showing prospector's homes in Colorado sometime between 1898 and 1905.

At right is another picture from the same company and time period, this one titled 'Aspen Silver Mines'. Both images were colorized and published as stereo views or postcards, adding to a romantic notion of mining that tended to downplay the physical hardships. Prospectors were often far from home, barely surviving financially, and at the mercy of the elements.

The magnificent photograph **below** is from inside the Bobtail Mine in Black Hawk Canyon. Published in August of 1898, it's a B.L. Singley image from the Keystone View Co that predates flash, and it was made into a stereograph view card. The Bobtail had been discovered back in 1859 and owed its longevity to Nathaniel Hill's ore smelter, which was erected in Black Hawk in 1868.

Chapter 7
A New Century

According to the Colorado Department of Local Affairs, the state had a population of 541,483 as it entered the new millennium. Life in Colorado was becoming more settled for people such as trader J.L. Niebergall. His log cabin store in Cripple Creek was expanding into a new stick-built addition in the c.1900 photograph **above** (titled 'a pioneer merchant' by the Detroit Photographic Co. Some sources list this image as earlier, perhaps '92 or '93.). According to the city's website, "in 1890, a ranch hand named Bob Womack discovered gold and Cripple Creek changed forever. By 1900, more than 50,000 people called the gold camp home. When the golden era ended in 1918, more than $300 million in gold had been mined in what would be the last great gold rush in North America." While Mr. Niebergall hammered in peace, there were some dramatic events taking place on the world stage including the Boxer Rebellion and the Boer War.

In June 1900, delegates for the upcoming Republican convention met in Philadelphia to choose a running mate for William McKinley, whose vice president, Garret Augustus Hobart, had died of heart disease at the age of 55 (he was the sixth VP to die in office). After Pennsylvania, Colorado was the second state to support the eventual nominee, Theodore Roosevelt, who was the governor of New York. Within a year, on September 14, 1901, Roosevelt would be sworn in as President of the United States following the assassination of McKinley.

The Denver Museum of Nature and Science (dmns.org) was founded in 1900. Thirty-two years previously, the naturalist Edwin Carter had migrated to Breckinridge to study Rocky Mountain animal life. He turned his log cabin into a virtual museum (shown **at right** in an unattributed image c.1875), filling it with Colorado bird and mammal specimens. The collection was moved to larger premises in 1900 and incorporated as the Colorado Museum of Natural History. In 1908, the collection was again moved, this time to a new structure in Denver's City Park. Since then there have been several major additions, including the Phipps Auditorium in 1940, the Gates Planetarium in 1968, an IMAX theater in 1983, a 187,000 square foot addition in 1987, and both the 12,850 square feet Leprino Family Atrium and the 5,000 square foot Anschutz Family Sky Terrace in 2002. The latter was designed as an open-air space for viewing the night sky over Denver's skyline, with the Rocky Mountains as a backdrop. That was a popular device among photographers who wished to give some scale to the mountains. **Below**, for example, is a c.1900 panorama of the Boulder skyline, by the Detroit Photographic Co.

Above: Edwin Carter

Not every town still gets to pose for photographs. **Below** is an image of Eureka, which today is nothing but a few foundations. The town started in 1860 and the railroad reached it in 1896. The Sunnyside Mill and a few saloons on Main Street sustained it until World War II, but it never really saw a boom. William Henry Jackson made this image around 1900, in the town's heyday.

And not every town turned to dust after the ore ran out. In 1900, there were 18,000 residents in Victor, a settlement at 9,708 feet on the southwest side of Pikes Peak. Today, with a population of about 400, the town has become a tourism destination and a center of the arts. There is even some new mining on Battle Mountain, a stone's throw north of town.

Below is a c.1900 panorama of Victor by William Henry Jackson, showing the downtown area and the shaft house of the Gold Coin Mine (the large building at center with the smoke stack).

Settlements across Colorado were growing exponentially. By 1900, Denver had become a major center of commerce and, with the notable exception of Salt Lake City, it was the focal point of a vast area that extended from California to Minnesota, and from Santa Fe to Canada. The city's population was well over 130,000 already, and would explode to 213,000 by the end of the decade. Roughly one in four residents of the state lived in the capital. (Today, the 12-county metro area is home to more than three million residents, and the U.S. Census Bureau estimated that the 2013 population of the state of Colorado was 5,268,367, up almost 5% since the 2010 national census.)

In the stereoscope **below**, made by Graves Photo in 1900, we are looking at 17th Street, with a jewelry store (Sam Mayer's Diamond Palace) on the right. The store's actual address was 1638 Larimer Street, but looking at photographic clues, it seems a lot like the clock was located on the

sidewalk at what is now Market and 17th, outside the Market Center building. The address there is 1624 Market Street. Either way, we're still looking southeast down 17th (only from a different block). By 1900, the city already had a large number of brick and stone edifices, a well-developed streetcar system, and a thriving shopping district. Bicycles were as popular then as they are today. Unfortunately, it would also seem that many of the buildings gave way to urban renewal over the years, changing the character of the streets and neighborhoods as people began to look up to steel and glass towers, both physically and figuratively.

In 1901, William Henry Jackson photographed Silverton (**below**). The city sits at an altitude of 9,318 feet, and its origins reach back to 1860 and the discovery of gold. It was platted in 1874 and the Denver & Rio Grande reached the site in 1882. Silverton was at its zenith during the first decade of the new century, with three railroads hauling ore into town to be smelted.

The main drag, Blair Street, was home to forty saloons and brothels. Today, the population is only about 500 and the last mine, the Sunnyside Gold, closed in 1991. But the city is very much alive as a tourism destination (silvertoncolorado.com). In summer, visitors ride the Durango & Silverton narrow gauge, and in winter there's extreme skiing and snowboarding on Silverton Mountain, and family winter sports at the Kendall Mountain ski resort.

About as far from Silverton as one can get and still be in Colorado, another outdoor playground was in the works. President Roosevelt had established the Medicine Bow Forest Reserve on the Wyoming side of the border on May 22nd 1902. It would eventually be expanded twice: in 1929, when Hayden National Forest was included, and again in 1959 with the addition of the Pole Mountain Unit. The name 'Medicine Bow' may have come from the hybrid language that was developed by Native Americans and trappers/mountain men, which contained elements of both tongues. The accepted origin is that some tribes used relatively rare mountain mahogany to fashion bows, and its harvest was a social occasion during which some healing took place. At some stage there was confusion between the terms 'making medicine' and 'making bow'. Medicine Bow became familiar to Easterners when Owen Wister located *The Virginian* there, and became part of the American lexicon when the novel was serialized for television.

On the Colorado side of the line, the Routt National Forest was established. It lies between Rocky Mountain National Park and Dinosaur National Monument, and is home to the Steamboat Springs ski area. It was named for Colonel John Routt, the last territorial governor and the first state governor of Colorado. The forest was set aside in 1905 and named in 1908, again by President Roosevelt. The Medicine Bow-Routt National Forest now includes more than two million acres in the states of Wyoming and Colorado, as Medicine Bow National Forest and Routt National Forest were combined with Thunder Basin National Grassland in 1995.

Above is a c.1920 image of a remote U.S. Forest Service toolbox located in the Routt National Forest, Colorado, showing tools and canned food inside. (National Photo Company)

Silverton wasn't the only breathtakingly beautiful valley to be developed, and to later become a tourism destination. **Below** is another William Henry Jackson image, this time showcasing the Hotel Colorado in Glenwood Springs, in 1901. The city is situated at the confluence of the Roaring Fork and Colorado Rivers, 180 miles west of Denver across the Divide.

Throughout its history, Glenwood Springs has been known for its medicinal hot sulfur springs and scenic beauty. The first homesteader, around 1882, was James Landis, who staked his claim at the confluence of the two rivers. Within a year or so, two more settlers, Isaac Cooper and Walter Devereux arrived and began developing the spot into a resort. When the railroads came in 1887, tourism took off in a big way. Soon, more attractions were added, including the Vapor Caves in 1892, the Hotel Colorado in 1893, and the Fairy Caves in 1896. People in Glenwood Springs didn't just rely on tourism, however: they also engaged in coal mining, farming and ranching. In the city's Linwood Cemetery, one can visit the grave of Doc Holliday, who finally succumbed to tuberculosis (TB) in November 1887. He's in bad company: Harvey Logan (Kid Curry, of the Butch Cassidy gang) also lies in Linwood. He bought his own ticket to eternity in 1904, after a train robbery near Parachute.

While the West is dotted with memorials to bandits and gunslingers, there are also a number of monuments to more enlightened heroes across Colorado. For example, on the 4th July 1904, a statue of the poet Robert Burns (1759-1796) was erected in City Park in Denver by the Caledonian Club. Sculpted by the Scots artist William Grant Stevenson, the figure stands ten feet tall atop a marble and granite base (**below**).

There is a shrine to the memory of cowboy, vaudeville performer, humorist, social commentator and motion picture actor Will Rogers in Colorado Springs. On the Cheyenne Mountain Zoo site, we learn that the structure was "built by Spencer Penrose between 1934 and 1937, [and] it stands dedicated to Will Rogers who died in a plane crash in 1935. The elevation of the shrine is 8,136 feet on the top deck and provides breathtaking views of Colorado Springs and the Pikes Peak Region". (cmzoo.org)

Buffalo Bill Cody's grave is near Golden, Colorado. He died of kidney failure on January 10th 1917 at his sister's home in Denver, one day after becoming a Catholic. His service was at the Elk's Lodge in Denver, and the ritual was in accordance with the order of the Masonic Lodge. His grave is on the side of Lookout Mountain, overlooking the plains. Cody was a genuine American hero: in 1872, he was awarded the Medal of Honor as a civilian Cavalry scout. (It was rescinded in 1917 and reinstated in 1989, as the rules changed with political winds). The Buffalo Bill Museum and Grave website is at buffalobill.org. Tourist attractions across the state experienced two distinct boosts – when rail service reached their respective towns, and when automobiles arrived. The vehicles shown in the image **below** were featured in a National Cash Register (NCR) ad, and they were photographed at the Felken Cycle Company in Denver in 1902.

One of the most startling images related to transportation around this time was the Cherrelyn coach, a railroad anomaly located in Denver. The popular tourist attraction was in business from 1883

to 1910, and only cost a dime. The horse pulled the car full of passengers a mile and a half up the hill from Hampden and Broadway to the stores at Cherryelyn. Then, it climbed aboard for the return trip! The outbound (uphill) portion lasted about a quarter of an hour, and the gravity-fed return only took three minutes. The horse car is now located at the Englewood Civic Center, about three miles south of downtown Denver.

A pioneer in her field, Frances Benjamin Johnston made the two photographs here in 1903. She was capturing the end of an era, although it did take some time for Colorado's horses and railroads to be replaced by automobiles. Building roads through remote areas of the Rockies was an engineering challenge and a huge expense.

Cars, too, were expensive and unreliable. However, narrow gauge track was already being phased out early in the new century, and standardization of the rail industry began to curtail many of the cost-cutting strategies that had placed passengers and freight in danger, but saved money. The result was that new track was more costly, and as some placer deposits and even shaft ore began to run out, the railroads began to reassess investment in hard-to-reach places. People kept on penetrating the mountains and, as each year passed, it became more logical to invest in roads and cars than mass transportation. But that was still down the road: in 1904, as we see in the image **below**, people still drove horse-drawn buggies.

This was the scene in Rocky Ford (southeast of Pueblo and close to La Junta) when people gathered for the annual Watermelon Day. The town is located near a bend of the Arkansas River and the celebration, which began in 1878, is still part of the Arkansas Valley Fair (arkvalleyfair.com), which the city claims is "the oldest continuous fair in the State of Colorado".

In the early years of the century, President Roosevelt (**below**, in 1905, addressing a crowd at Colorado Springs in a photograph by H.C. White) had quite an impact on Colorado. Over a period of five years he signed legislation creating the White River, Gunnison, Leadville, Pike's Peak, San Juan, Park Range, San Isabel, Wet Mountains, Cochetopa, Montezuma, Uncompahgre, Holy Cross, La Sal and Fruita Forest Reserves. In 1906, he signed an Act of Congress creating Mesa Verde National Park and the following year he signed an order creating Arapaho National Forest.

Speaking of politicians, Saint Patrick's Day in 1905 was an especially strange one for Colorado. It was the day the gubernatorial election results were made public, and Alva Adams won. But Republicans, who still controlled the state legislature, insisted that significant fraud and corruption had taken place to steal the election from incumbent James Peabody, and they voted to remove Adams, a Democrat, from office. But they also didn't want Peabody in power because of his awful record, so he was asked to resign immediately in favor of his lieutenant governor, Jesse McDonald. Much of the criticism of Peabody was related to his handling of a strike by miners at Cripple Creek. At the time, there were several industrial actions by mining unions trying to improve the wages and working conditions of their members. There were strikes in the gold and silver mines at Clear Creek, Cripple Creek and Telluride, and in the coalmines of Las Animas County.

On several occasions, Peabody called out the Colorado National Guard, and used force to maintain order. The strategy was seen by most Coloradoans as overkill, and unfair.

About a hundred days after the election, the people of Pueblo were in a much more light-hearted mood. On 4th July, they witnessed Eunice Padfield and her horse diving from a high tower in an incredible act of daring. Photographer Clifford Holmboe captured the event in the photograph **at left**. That same year (1905), Holmboe also captured the image below of the American Beet factory in Rocky Ford, on its fifth anniversary.

Sugar beet would prove to be quite important to the economy of eastern Colorado over the next few decades.

Chapter 8
Native Coloradoans

What is now the state of Colorado was once home to a series of diverse and highly successful Native cultures that included members of the Jicarilla Apache, Arapaho, Cheyenne and Ute nations, and the Pueblo and Shoshone/Bannock tribes. There were also some Comanche, Kiowa and Navajo presences at various times. Today, there are only two federally recognized tribes within the state's boundaries.

The Southern Ute are based in and around Ignacio, and are the most numerous at 1,400 members. The Ute Mountain Ute, with headquarters in Towaoc, numbered 1,087 in the 2010 census.

Most of the celebrated Native figures in Colorado's history were Ute, including the chiefs Ouray, Buckskin Charley, Severo (shown with his family on the previous page in a Nast image for the Detroit Publishing Company, c.1899), and Ignacio.

This image by John Jarvis shows a group of Ute men and women in Colorado c.1893.

By the time of the first contact with Europeans, Colorado's Ute tribes lived primarily in the central and western mountain valleys and the Comanche, Cheyenne, Arapaho, and Kiowa hunted on the eastern plains. By then, the Pueblo inhabitants of Mesa Verde had already abandoned their cliff dwellings (see Chapter 1), and headed south.

This Ute mother and child were photographed either near Eggleston Lake, east of Grand Junction, or they were from there. The portrait was made by Samuels and Mays of Meeker, which is about 100 miles north of Grand Junction, c. 1902.

The Utes were among the very earliest Native people to domesticate and use horses in North America. There is some evidence of this practice dating back to the end of the sixteenth century, although a majority opinion dates acquisition to the 1600s. Utes spoke (and speak) a Shoshonean dialect. The tribe seems to have originated in what is now Utah (named after them), and Colorado, and there is no other migratory provenance. A non-cohesive alliance, they are comprised of numerous bands including the Mouache (Moache) who occupied foothills from what is now Denver south to the New Mexico border, and the Caputa (Capote) band from the San Luis Valley. Today, these two bands make up the majority of the Southern Ute Tribe. Other bands include the Weenuchiu (Weeminuche), Uncompahgre, Parianuche, Yamparika (Yamperika), Uintah (Uinta), Pahvant (Pah Vant), Timonogots (Timanogots), Taviwach, Sanpits (San Pitch), Moanumts, Tumpanawach, Sheberetch and Comumba (Cumumba). The language has an oral tradition, so spelling is not uniform.

A land without intense cultivation can only support a limited population, and game moves quickly, so the Ute learned early on that smaller, more mobile bands and family units were far more efficient than large tribal congregations. Small nomadic pods also had a lesser impact on the environment, allowing the country to refresh itself and keep pace with a band's needs.

Among the bounty that nature provided were elk, antelope, deer, fish, tobacco, chokecherries, pine bark, wild raspberries, lilies, yampa (a carrot), gooseberries, prickly pear cactus, buffalo berries, amaranth (a high protein seed grain, and in some cases a leafy vegetable), wild onion, wild potato, rice grass, peppermint and dandelion. Some cooking was done in fire pits with heated rocks and layers of grass. Bear root (osha) was used to treat colds, aches and other ailments. Cured hides became homes, clothing and moccasins. Sumac and willow were worked into exquisite basketry. Quills decorated prized beadwork. Yucca became soap and also a weaving material for baskets, rope and mats.

A complex belief system and oral culture emerged over the centuries. The tribes still celebrate spring with the traditional Bear Dance, a gift from the hibernating ursidae who dance with joy upon waking from a winter sleep. Much of the Ute culture has changed since that first contact with the Spanish. Europeans added domestic animals, knives and other technology to Ute life, but they also brought smallpox, diphtheria, cholera, measles and other diseases. And they brought a culture based on material gain, which often translated into a disregard for both human life and nature, and an insatiable appetite for other people's land and resources.

This portrait of Chief Ignacio (1828–1913) and his handsome colt was by Frank Balster of Durango, 1904. The chief was Weeminuche.

This was mystifying at first, as the Utes believed that they didn't own the land, but that the land owned them. The Spanish also enslaved some Ute bands, forcing them to work as field hands and domestic servants.

For much of the eighteenth century, the Ute and Comanche nations fought a three-generation war. About this time, the acquisition of more Spanish horses meant that larger and faster game was now prey, and longer annual migrations were possible. Bison increasingly became part of the tribes' diet, and provided a rich source of materials for the manufacture of domestic goods. The influence of European values translated into a desire for wealth, often measured in terms of the number of horses owned. A trickle of guns began entering the Ute world, at first as a means of hunting and very quickly becoming a weapon of aggression, and defense. Europeans coveted the timber, water and minerals of the mountains, and as soon as gold was discovered, the Ute homeland began to shrink rapidly, dramatically and violently. The first of several treaties with the United States was signed in 1849, the same year as the San Francisco gold rush. During the Civil War, an 1863 treaty surrendered all mineral and land rights in the San Luis valley. And in 1868 a reservation was established for the Southern Utes that included the western half of Colorado and amounted to 56 million acres. The government's largess didn't last long. As soon as substantial deposits of gold and silver were discovered in the San Juans, the United States decided to renegotiate. Utes regard the Brunot Treaty, which was ratified by the US in 1874, as the ultimate fraud that tricked them out of their traditional lands. They apparently believed that they were granting mining rights in the San Juan Mountain region, but ended up losing millions of acres of tribal lands.

Portrait of a Ute bridegroom by C.E. Emory, 1906.

A pivotal event for the Utes became known as the Meeker Massacre. In 1870 the journalist Nathanial Meeker had founded a Utopian settlement called Union Colony in Greeley. Meeker eventually became an Indian agent and, in 1878 was appointed the US Agent at White River. At this time, there was a strong push by the government to 'civilize' the Utes, to have them abandon their nomadic lifestyle, settle down, raise crops and build schools. In that spirit, Meeker had the Ute's horse racing track plowed under, and wanted the tribe to kill off some of their herd because the horses ate too much and occupied too much pasture. After an argument in which Meeker was struck, he called for Army intervention. A force of about 170 men, led by Major Tom Thornburgh, approached the agency. A Ute delegation intercepted them and asked that only a representative enter the agency, leaving the troops at some distance: they were at the time mindful of the Sand Creek Massacre.

This panorama of a Ute camp was too wide for the page, so it is presented in two halves.
The Stewart Brothers made it in 1913, at the Garden of the Gods.

The major decided to proceed anyway, and before he could reach the settlement the Utes killed Meeker and ten men who worked at the agency, and took women and children as hostages. Among them were Meeker's wife and adult daughter. Then, a war party attacked the soldiers. The major and thirteen of his men were killed and the remaining troops entrenched in defensive positions. A force of 350 troopers under Colonel David Merritt put down the uprising and rescued Thornburgh's men at the battle of Milk Creek. Chief Ouray, who had not been involved, negotiated the release of the captives with his wife's help. In 1880 the US Congress passed the Ute Removal Act to remove the Utes from Colorado to reservations in eastern Utah, and confiscate another twelve million acres of their land. Despite his band's non-involvement and his efforts at peace, Chief Ouray and his people were removed. He died shortly thereafter on a reservation in Utah.

The final act of empire occurred in 1895 with passage of the Hunter Act, which had the effect of privatizing communal lands and making them much easier for individuals or families to sell. Just prior to its passage, the Southern Ute reservation was created, which restricted the tribe to an area that is about the size of the current Denver metro – just 15 miles wide and 110 miles long. Although seven rivers run through the reservation, control of this resource was rarely left in Ute hands.

As happened with other tribes, the government set up boarding schools and immersed young people in the dominant culture in an effort to eradicate traditional

The caption on this beautiful National Photo Company image, dated between 1909 and 1932, reads only: "Indian with two tepees beside a lake in Rocky Mountain National Park, Colorado."

ways. And as it did in most cases, the policy only worked to create generations of young people who belonged to neither world, instead of both or either. **Below** is a photograph of the Southern Ute Boarding School's Boys' Dormitory, which was located at Ouray and Capote Streets in Ignacio. The image was made about 1930 by a HABS photographer (probably Clayton Fraser).

Almost a century after the Hunter Act, in 1988, Congress passed the Colorado Ute Indian Water Rights Settlement Act, which deeded some traditional water rights back to the tribe. However, the water sits in manmade Lake Nighthorse (a couple of miles from Durango), which was filled in 2011. The lake was named in honor of former United States Senator Ben Nighthorse Campbell (Republican, Colorado). At the time of publication, it seems no federal funds have yet been made available to transport water via pipelines from the reservoir to the two Ute reservations.

There are many positive signs for the road ahead. There is, for example, a strong effort to preserve the Ute language. In 2000, the Southern Ute Tribal Academy opened its doors to children up to sixth grade, and the curriculum includes a comprehensive Ute language program. Now called the Southern Ute Indian Montessori Academy (southernute-nsn.gov/private-education), the school has expanded its agenda and is a cultural and educational beacon for the nation. What is ironic is that the classrooms are beside the boarding school in Ignacio where teachers once washed children's mouths with soap for speaking their Ute language.

And there are good economic signposts, too. Ute Mountain Casino is located eleven miles South of Cortez (utemountaincasino.com), and is owned by the Ute Mountain Ute Tribe.

Chapter 9
Politicians and Power

In 1904, work began on the Shoshone Hydroelectric Generating Station in Glenwood Springs. It came online in 1909, delivering electric power to the Denver area 150 miles to the east. The plant is still in use and is capable of producing up to 15 MW of electricity. To run its two units, water is diverted from the Colorado River and then returned to the river after use. The turbines depend on the flow of the river, rather than a trapped body of water.

In 1905, the Cheesman Dam was completed, harnessing the waters of the South Platte for use in Denver. It was named for Walter S. Cheesman, a Denver businessman who pioneered water management in the city. When it opened, it was the tallest dam in the world (221 feet above the streambed, which is about 3/4 of the length of a football field). In 1973, the curved concrete masterpiece was designated a National Historic Civil Engineering Landmark.

That year, Teddy Roosevelt spent some time in Colorado. **At right**, he is shown in a H.C. White image with two fellow hunters identified as Dr. Chapman and Philip Stewart, getting ready to head into the mountains to hunt bear. **On the next page** is an image by Philip Stewart (of Scribner's Magazine) showing the group returning with a large black bear. This was not the trip that gave rise to Teddy Bears: that had happened in Mississippi a couple of years earlier. This hunt took place on Divide Creek near New Castle, and Roosevelt stayed at the Colorado Hotel in nearby Glenwood Springs.

In January 1906, the first Western Livestock Show took place in Denver. The organizing group was incorporated as the Western Stock Show Association and the show has taken place every year

since, except for 1915 when a hoof and mouth disease epidemic prohibited travel. Today it is known as the National Western Stock Show and Rodeo (nationalwestern.com). In 1931, a rodeo was added, and in 1942 the WPA built a huge barn for the event. Two years later, the Quarter Horse show and sale made its first appearance. In 1952, the Denver Coliseum was dedicated just in time for the 46th National Western. In 1991 a new Expo Hall and stadium were added and in 1995 the Events Center, a massive equestrian arena, opened. In 2006, the show celebrated its centenary. Attendance that year was a little improved from the first year's 15,000 visitors. A hundred years down the road, the event attracted an immense crowd of 726,972 for the 16-day show!

That February, coinage operations began at the Denver Mint. And also in 1906, an engineering feat of extraordinary compass took place on Mount McClellan. Edward Wilcox's Argentine Central narrow gauge line reached the summit at 13,587 feet, making it the highest altitude ever reached in the United States by a non-rack (no cogs) railway. In July of 1908, the Democratic National Convention was held in Denver and it nominated William Jennings Bryan as the party's candidate for President of the United States. It was Bryan's third bid for the office, and he ultimately lost to Teddy Roosevelt's handpicked nominee, William Howard Taft. The Electoral College vote was pretty one-sided at 321 to 162. The convention was held in the Municipal Auditorium, and was the first time either party had convened in a Western state. It would be a full century until Denver hosted its next Democratic National Convention, in 2008.

The event was only the second in history to allow women delegates. There were two, and one of them, Mary Bradford, was from Colorado. Her father was a noted New York lawyer, and Ms.

Bradford was later appointed Colorado's Superintendent of Public Instruction (today, the Commissioner of Education). The Auditorium building (**at left**, during construction, from the George Grantham Bain collection) had been designed by architect Robert Willison, and was opened on July 7th, which was actually the first day of the Convention. Today the building, after extensive renovations, is part of the Denver Performing Arts Complex, which is home to the Ellie Caulkins Opera House.

Below is a panoramic view of the plaza and esplanade at Lakeside Park, taken that summer by H.H. Tammen of Denver. At the time, the Chairman of the Democratic National Committee was Norman Mack (**at right**, with Mrs. Mack in another Bain image), who was the editor and publisher of the *Buffalo Daily Times*.

Mack was actually a native of Ontario, and had been a delegate from New York in both 1896 and 1900. In 1912, he would go on to be a speaker at that convention, in part because by then he was serving as the state chair. Mack sold his newspaper in 1929 for six million dollars (about $138m in 2014). He died in 1932 and is interred at Forest Lawn in Buffalo.

In that 1908 election, a school principal turned lawyer from Leadville, Edward Taylor, was elected to his first term in Congress. He would remain in office for the next sixteen sessions (thirty-two years), until his death in 1941. Neither Mr. Taylor nor his constituents approved of term limits.

In 1909, acrobat Ivy Baldwin made a record-setting tightrope walk over South Boulder (now Eldorado) Canyon, traveling 582 feet at a height of 555 feet. The location of the walk is now a state park in Eldorado Springs, close to Boulder. In 1910, aviator Ralph Greenley Johnstone was the first American pilot to ever die in an airplane crash, and he did so in Denver.

On June 1st 1913, there was an unveiling of a new statue of Kit Carson in Trinidad, and the Kit Carson Park was dedicated that day too (**above**, photo by Almeron Newman). It's located at the corner of Kansas Avenue and San Pedro Street, overlooking what was once part of the Santa Fe Trail.

There is a state park named after Carson near Taos, New Mexico, and the Kit Carson Home and Museum is in Taos. The Kit Carson Memorial Hospital is in Burlington, which is the county seat of Kit Carson County, Colorado. And there is, of course, the town of Kit Carson in Cheyenne County in eastern Colorado. His life has also inspired many books, television shows and movies.

That December, in the infamous 1913 Blizzard, Denver received the greatest amount of snowfall ever from a single storm (45.7 inches). However, Georgetown, an hour west of the capital, took the state record in the storm with 86 inches. Georgetown is 3-1/2 miles east of Silver Plume in the Clear Creek Canyon, and the towns are home to the Georgetown Loop Historic Mining & Railroad Park, which offers train rides and mine tours (georgetownlooprr.com).

The Colorado Coalfield War

1914 was a sad year in Colorado. That April, the state's National Guard killed 19 striking coal miners, 2 women, and 11 children in what has come to be known as the Ludlow Massacre. Bain News Service created the photographs over the next three pages. **At left**, some miners' bodies lay on the railroad tracks for days because the National Guard wouldn't allow their removal. **Below**, several newspaper reporters traveled

through the battleground under a flag of truce.

There had been considerable unrest among many of the state's miners for several years, and things began to boil over when a United Mine Workers organizer was murdered in the fall of 1913. Coal miners at the Colorado Fuel & Iron Corporation, which was owned by John D. Rockefeller and members of his family, went out on strike in late September and stayed out until December 1914. The work was hard and very dangerous (the mortality rate in Colorado was 7 per 1,000 annually, which was more than twice the national average), and the pay was extremely low.

Miners were usually paid in company scrip, which could only be used at the company's store. They were paid by tonnage, so any work that didn't result in actual coal, such as taking time to shore up tunnels or fix equipment, was usually unpaid. That may have been a large part of the lack of safety, and high mortality rate.

The owners quickly began to evict striking workers from company-owned housing, and tent camps sprung up that winter near the gates of several mines. The locations were deliberate, and intended to deter strikebreakers (non-union workers, often called 'scabs'). Soon, mine guards began firing randomly into the camps, and the miners dug trenches to protect their families from bullets. The scene was in many ways mindful of the trench warfare that was about to rage in the poppy fields of France. The Rockefellers' representatives even commissioned an armored car to be built on site. In October, Governor Elias Ammons called out the National Guard, but those in command were very much on the side of the owners.

It was a long winter and in March of 1914, the body of a 'scab' worker was found near a camp called Forbes. The National Guard commander, Adjutant-General John Chase, ordered the destruction of that camp and the eviction of miners from all of the camps, even though most of them were on private property.

On April 20th, the Guard under a Lieutenant Linderfelt attacked the largest camp, which was called Ludlow and housed about 1,200 people. An all-day battle ensued, with armed miners firing back. As the sun began to set, one of the miners' leaders, Louis Tikas, was beaten by Linderfelt and was later found shot to death. Then the Guard set fire to the tents, killing women and children (the photograph **above** shows the aftermath).

Over the next ten days, a virtual war raged along a front that extended from Walsenburg to Trinidad. It only ended when President Woodrow Wilson sent in regular troops who disarmed both sides. Even though dozens of people died in the episode (estimates range from 60 to 100), and some 400 miners were arrested, only one man was convicted of murder and the verdict was eventually overturned. The only Guardsman who was convicted was Linderfelt, who had his wrist slapped. Congress held an investigation, and in time Rockefeller softened his views and improved conditions in his mines.

The image above shows six men in military uniform, identified as, from left, Lieutenants J.K. Hume and J.P. Wheeler, Captains E. Portner, G. P. Rodney and T.D. Woodson, and Lieutenant Ned Miller. It is not known whether they were National Guard members who attacked the Ludlow camp, or part of the federal force that eventually disarmed the Guard. (Our guess is the latter, based on many images of regulars and militia.)

South Dakota Senator and presidential nominee George McGovern wrote his doctoral dissertation on the Ludlow Massacre, which he published as *The Great Coalfield War*. And in 2013, Colorado Governor John Hickenlooper signed an executive order to create the Ludlow Centennial Commemoration Commission, designed to enhance awareness of the massacre and the miners struggle for a living wage and safer working conditions.

Quality of Life Improves

It's hard to imagine that, with federal troops patrolling the streets of Trinidad, the United States government would have time for any other business in Colorado. But on January 26th 1915, Congress created Rocky Mountain National Park, which was dedicated in Horseshoe Park that September. The next month, Dinosaur National Monument was created in Moffat County, with one part of the park, the Dinosaur Quarry, located in Utah. And around this time, work also began on the construction of the Fitzsimons Army Hospital in Aurora.

The hospital was dedicated in the autumn of 1918, just as the war in Europe came to a close. The site was 577 acres, and the citizens who supported the project and recommended it to the War Department stressed how Denver's climate was an asset in the treatment of tuberculosis. Secretary of State John Kerry was born in the facility when his father, a Foreign Service officer, was undergoing treatment for TB in 1943. Army involvement ended in 1999, and most of the facility is now known as the Fitzsimons Life Science District. It is "the center of Colorado's bioscience practice and research community and is one of the largest bioscience real estate developments in the country". The site is also home to the University of Colorado's Anschutz Medical Campus, which includes the University of Colorado Schools of Medicine, Pharmacy, Nursing and Dentistry, the Colorado School of Public Health, and a graduate school for biological and biomedical sciences.

Miners at Idaho Springs, Co, working by candlelight in pit, mine car in background. (S.A. Noyes, 1915)

In 1918, the Denver Art Museum came into being. It had been founded in 1893 as the Denver Artists' Club, and after an itinerant beginning opened galleries on 14th Avenue Parkway in 1949. A center for children's art activities was added in the early 1950s and in 1971 the museum opened its "24-sided, two-towered North Building by Ponti in collaboration with James Sudler Associates of Denver". On October 7, 2006, the Denver Art Museum nearly doubled in size when it opened one of the country's most unique structures, the Frederic C. Hamilton Building. Today, the Art Museum is one of the largest of its kind between Chicago and the West Coast, with a collection of more than 70,000 works of art divided between 10 permanent collections.

Chapter 10
The Teens and Twenties

The 1910 census had revealed that the state's population was 799,044. In July that year, President Taft signed legislation creating the Colorado National Forest, which would be renamed the Roosevelt

The "Unsinkable" Molly Brown

National Forest in 1932. The following year, he did the same for Colorado National Monument. And that year (1911), the Mountain States Telephone & Telegraph Co. was born. Theodore Vail was the president of American Telephone & Telegraph (AT&T) from 1907 to 1919, and he combined Colorado Telephone (and its subsidiary Tri-State) with Rocky Mountain Bell to form what would eventually become today's Qwest Communications. (Vale is sometimes confused with Frederick Vaille, who had been one of the original investors in an American Bell Telephone Company franchise named the Denver Telephone Dispatch Company, back in 1879.)

In 1885 Margaret Brown, the eighteen-year-old daughter of Irish parents, had arrived in Leadville with her sister Mary Ann, and her sister's husband Jack Landrigan. The couple opened a blacksmith's shop, and Maggie worked in the carpet and draperies room at Daniels and Fisher Mercantile in Leadville until she married James (JJ) Brown in 1886. She became a Suffragette as he became one of the most successful mine owners in the region. In 1894, they moved to Denver and Maggie (shown **at left** in a c.1900 portrait by Bain News Service), worked ceaselessly for those in need. She was instrumental in creating what eventually would become the United States juvenile justice system, and she ran for the Senate before women had a vote.

In 1912, Maggie Brown boarded the Titanic at Cherbourg, France. During the disaster at sea on the morning of the 15th April 1912, she was a source of encouragement and courage, helping all around her. Afterward, Mrs. Brown used her newfound fame to bring weight to campaigns supporting labor rights, women's rights, children's literacy and historic preservation. She passed away in 1932 in New York, fondly remembered by thousands of ordinary people whose lived she had touched, and greatly enhanced. Hollywood christened her as the Unsinkable Molly Brown, although she had never been known as Molly. She was an American heroine, and an example of everything that is wonderful about this country.

In 1912, the Colorado Mountain Club (cmc.org) was formed. As one of the state's oldest organizations, CMC focuses on conservation, advocacy, youth and adult education, and outdoor recreation adventures. The club "works to ensure that current and future generations have the access and ability to enjoy Colorado's open spaces and outdoor activities".

Indoor activities were doing well around the state, too. This Byers Photo/J.C. Anderson & Co. photograph **at left** shows men in a Telluride saloon gambling at the card table, with a roulette wheel in the foreground. A second card game is in progress at the back of the room. In this uniquely Western scene shot between 1910 and 1920, the county sheriff leans against the bar at right. There are elk mounts above the backbar, a nude woman's portrait on the back wall, and the only African American in the photo is polishing the brass foot rail. Note the papered ceiling, regulator clock, ornate Victorian wood stove, and the brass spittoons behind the foot rail. The light bulbs are irregular, suggesting they were hand blown.

Denver was also doing well. The 1915 skyline at top was by Haines Photo Co. of Conneaut, Ohio. Carol Highsmith shot the panorama below some seven decades later (1980s). For orientation, in the top photo the capitol dome is located about center and below, it is at the lower right.

Speaking of Capitols, here's an interesting side-note about a Congressman. Jeremiah Haralson (**at left** by Matthew Brady, c.1876) was born into slavery in 1846 in Georgia, and in 1875 he became a one-term member of the House, representing Alabama's 1st Congressional District. He was the first African American member of the Alabama House of Representatives in 1870 as a Republican, and was elected to the state Senate in 1872. After Congress, he worked in various government positions and farmed a little. He was living in Selma in 1912 and subsequently moved in turn to Texas, Oklahoma and finally Colorado where he took up coal mining. According to Congressional records, Jeremiah Haralson was killed by "a wild animal" while hunting near Denver in 1916 (a year after the skyline photo above was taken).

140

Back in 1905, the name of the White River National Reserve had been changed to "National Forest", a designation that allowed forestry and other resource management and harvest. By the

1930s, the area was becoming a popular skiing destination. The image **at left** shows a government-paid hunter (on the right) in the Forest, working on coyote and other management directives. The man on the left is wearing a Ranger's badge. (National Photo Company, between 1909 and 1932).

Below, in another image by the same company and in the same time period, a group of trail riders enjoy a guided trek in Rocky Mountain National

Park.

In 1919 the actor Douglas Fairbanks (born in Denver in 1883) founded United Artists along with girlfriend Mary Pickford (whom he married in 1920) and friends Charlie Chaplin and D.W. Griffith. He had a stellar career until 1934 onscreen, and was an astute and successful businessman until his untimely death in 1939 (he was just 56). Fairbanks was a founding member of the Motion Picture Academy and hosted the first Oscars in 1929.

By 1920, the state's population was approaching one million.

In May of 1921, Colorado's first commercially licensed radio station, KFKA, hit the airwaves. It was only the second station west of the Mississippi, and the fifth in the nation.

In June of 1921, a strong thunderstorm delivered torrential rains about ten miles west of Pueblo, flooding the Arkansas River. Another storm cell deluged Fountain Creek, thirty miles to the north. When the high water from both events reached Pueblo simultaneously, the result was a heartbreaking loss of life and horrendous damage to property. In all, some fifteen hundred people perished, and another three thousand refugees had to be fed each day at the Elks Lodge until relief agencies and federal help arrived.

That year in Alamosa, the first students enrolled in a new teacher training college called Adams State Normal School. In 2014, Adams State University enjoyed an all-time high enrollment of 3,701 students and has both masters and doctoral programs.

Between 1922 and 1927, the six-mile long Moffat Tunnel was drilled through James Peak, bridging the Continental Divide at about 9,200 elevation some fifty miles west of Denver. A much smaller tunnel was bored first, and this was then used for access to the larger project at various locations. That meant work could occur in several places simultaneously. The small tunnel was turned into an aqueduct (water supply line) for Denver after the rail tunnel opened.

On October 17th 1929, the Denver Municipal Airport (called Stapleton International Airport from 1944 until 1995) was dedicated. It was the precursor to today's Denver International Airport (DIA), which at 53 square miles is the largest airport in the United States.

In 1930, the state's population was 1,035,791 and even though many states lost numbers during the lean years, by 1940 Colorado was home to 1,123,296 residents. Even in the worst of times, people clung to art. **At left** is a 1934 shot of the Central City Opera House in Gilpin County, taken by HABS photographer Bernal Wells. Today, the historic 1878 structure is still home to a professional summer opera festival (PH: 303-292-6500).

Chapter 11
Sugarbeet and Dust

According to the American Sugarbeet Growers' Association, more than 4.5 million tons of sugar is produced each year in the US from sugarbeets, and beet sugar still represents 54% of domestic sugar production in the U.S. The Colorado Sugarbeet Growers' Association is based in Greeley, where a factory was opened in 1902, a year after a plant in Loveland went online.

A similar plant was located in Longmont and was operational from 1905 until 1980. The Greeley factory (**at left**, in an E.W. Kelley image from 1908 showing the filter presses) was in business for an entire century, only closing in 2002. In the 1970s and '80s, pressure from other sources began to erode the sugarbeet industry, including cane sugar and the emergence of high fructose corn syrup. In 1985, the Great Western Sugar Company declared bankruptcy. Growers' cooperatives took over some plants, but over the next couple of decades the Colorado sugarbeet industry continued to shrink. The last operational factory in the state is located in Fort Morgan. It was erected in 1906, and like many other plants, the farmers who supplied it also created irrigation systems. Those systems now support other harvests, and they are an essential part of the state's infrastructure.

Many of the photographs from this period depict people and situations that may look a little grim in today's affluent economy. It's important to remember that times were tough during the first half of the twentieth century, and the sugarbeet industry helped to keep families going through a period that saw two world wars, the Dust Bowl and the Great Depression. Children, especially, had it hard. Families were forced to rely on even small children's contributions, just to provide enough food for subsistence. **Below**, Mexican beet workers erected a temporary home near Rocky Ford in 1915. The photograph was made by Lewis Wickes Hine, a Wisconsin-born sociologist and activist who used his camera to defend children's rights, and in doing so helped change America's child labor laws. In 1908, Hine was asked to become a photographer for the National Child Labor Committee (NCLC) and, through the next decade, he documented child labor across the US, and especially in the South.

It was hard work producing and harvesting beets, but the industry had an immense impact on eastern Colorado. This lowly root encouraged farmers to settle on the land, provided jobs for both local and immigrant farm workers, dramatically increased the value of the land, supported the growth of towns and schools, and even provided cattle feed to new feedlots.

The next few photographs give some insight into the lives of the people who harvested beets, especially the transient workers who were often new immigrants.

At **top left** is a Hines image from 1915 showing "eleven-year old Elizabeth who has been working in the sugar beets near Ordway, Colorado, for one year. The family moved here from

Southern Russia three years ago. She said: 'I don't like the work so much'". Ordway is straight east of Pueblo, and about fifteen miles north of Rocky Ford.

Below right are "the summer quarters of a beet worker's family on a Colorado farm near Starling". The city's name should probably read Sterling, which is in the northeast corner of the state, about 38 miles down the South Platte river from the beet factory at Brush. One of the last confrontations between the Cavalry and the Cheyenne took place there in 1869, at the Battle of Summit Springs. Chief Tall Bull and his Cheyenne Dog Soldiers had been raiding in Kansas.

Colonel Eugene Carr was sent to take care of the problem. Carr had at his command 244 men of the 5th Cavalry and 50 Pawnee Scouts. Chief Tall Bull was among the first casualties, shot by Major Frank North. Of the 35 Cheyenne deaths, the Pawnee scouts killed thirty people. Among the dead were 24 warriors: the rest were women and children. The next day the civilian scout Buffalo Bill Cody shot one more Cheyenne warrior who was fleeing on Tall Bull's horse. No soldiers died.

At left is Hine's photograph of the Jungle in Fort Collins, the section in which the beet workers lived when they were not away working the beets. In Greeley, the segregated section was called The Pansy Bed, because of the varied and vivid coloring of homes, and in Sterling it was called Petersburg. Hines described the image below this way: "The prairie-wagon home of a family of itinerant beet workers, now camped near Ft. Collins, Colo. Street family.

"The children 7- 8- 10- and 12 work steadily and I saw the tiny girl pulling beets after sunset on the following Sunday, and they had not yet finished. The father told me 'We got squeezed out of the mountains'. One of the neighbors said they has been chased out because they wouldn't send their children to school."

The heart-wrenching image below is "six-year old Jo, pulling beets for his parents on a farm near Sterling", again by Hines. Many older Americans who grew up on farms remember helping out the family by weeding, or perhaps feeding stock or milking. Now, less than 1% of us farm.

Jack Allison of the FSA made this image, which he noted as "a girl of six who has full charge of her boy brother. Great Western Sugar Company's beet sugar workers' colony at Hudson, Colorado." The challenge is to look at these photographs in the context of their time (1938), rather than applying today's social norms. Their mother had no choice but to work: there were no food stamps until 1964 (with a limited exception from 1939-43 during the war). On the next page is an Allison photograph of men loading sugarbeets in Colorado in 1938.

Colorado was not spared the impact of the Dust Bowl. On the next page are two images of terrifying storms in 1936. The top photograph by J.H. Ward of the FSA is titled "dust storm in

Colorado" and was possibly taken near Lamar in the southeast corner of the state. D.L. Kernodle took the lower one near Springfield, in Baca County, south of Lamar.

It's difficult to imagine the way a parent might have felt watching these walls of dirt approaching, knowing that incipient fine particles would discover a way through the walls and windows of a house, and into children's lungs and throats.

Southeast Colorado averaged only about 12 inches of moisture annually during the 30s. The drought meant there was nothing growing, so when the wind blew it took the topsoil. Dust storms started about 1930 and grew in both intensity and frequency each year until the peak in 1937. It was, in essence, the genesis of a new desert. Animals died in the fields, trains ground to a standstill, fences disappeared under drifts and people built tents inside their homes, eating and sleeping under damp sheets. Grasshoppers arrived in huge waves, removing every last vestige of vegetation. And then there would be an infrequent cloudburst, delivering so much rain that flash floods washed away the soil, clogging creeks and drains and piling sediment into ditches and rivers. The Dust Bowl extended from southeastern Colorado through the western half of Kansas and northeastern New Mexico, and all the way down to the panhandles of Texas and Oklahoma.

What was especially painful was that the Dust Bowl occurred in the middle of the worst economic depression the country has ever seen, so national resources were stretched to their limits and there was limited help available for the farmers of eastern Colorado.

Several New Deal efforts provided loans to farmers and helped keep local banks solvent, and others paid for spraying poison on the grasshoppers. There were also food allotments, and many WPA projects that provided employment, especially for young men. Local relief efforts through counties, churches and community programs were nothing short of heroic.

A new way to treat the land emerged from lessons learned in the 30s. Settlement of government lands in the West essentially ground to a halt. The practice of plowing prairies virtually disappeared. Grazing permits for public lands became more restrictive and more often enforced, and were used to maintain and improve grassland. The Land Utilization Program (LUP), passed in 1934, was designed to prevent what President Franklin Roosevelt called the formation of a "man-made Sahara" in the middle of America.

But all of that didn't prevent four of every ten farm families in Baca County packing up and leaving during the decade. Many went to California, but there were other families who traveled the other direction. Migrant workers from Mexico, Oklahoma and Texas drove north to work in the

sugarbeet fields, and were astounded when the reached the state's southern border. Colorado's governor, Edwin Johnson, had declared martial law on April 18th 1936, and had stationed National Guard troops on the New Mexico line to turn back migrant workers both on trains and on the roads. Arthur Rothstein made the image at left that summer, showing two National Guardsmen manning a checkpoint on an ungraded road. (The sign by the tent is unrelated and just reads "No machines with lugs permitted on this road".)

The drought ended with the decade, and by then the national economy was recovering, in part due to an increase in arms manufacturing as a result of events in Europe. Britain and France were at war with Nazi Germany, and in 1937 Japan had invaded China. It wouldn't be long before Colorado left the dust and Depression behind, and began to send her sons around the world in defense of democracy.

In May 1936, planning began for a WPA/CCC project at the Red Rocks Amphitheatre. The somewhat abstract and intriguing view **at left** is from the Carol M. Highsmith Archive, and was taken between 1980 and 2006. The horseshoe shaped open-air theatre sits in a 640-acre park that hosts flora and fauna from both the Rocky Mountains and the Great Plains. The venue was originally the vision of John Brisben Walker, and then of George Cranmer who was the manager of Denver's city parks. Although construction would take the next twelve years, the facility was dedicated and opened to the public on June 15th, 1941. The first concert was on Easter Sunday in 1947. The theatre seats 9,525 attendees and its elevation of 6,450 feet has caused many musicians to comment on its acoustics. The thin air combines with the containment, reflection and shaping of notes created by a pair of three hundred-foot monoliths (called Ship Rock and Creation Rock) to deliver a unique and exquisite sound.

The next year saw the beginnings of another WPA project, Lowry Field. Originally located near East 38th Avenue and Dahlia Street, it was relocated to its final site near East 6th Avenue and Quebec Street with funds first authorized in 1937. The base expanded dramatically during World War II when bomber aircrews were trained there, and after the war it was used to train missile specialists. From 1953 to 1955, Lowry became President Dwight D. Eisenhower's 'Summer White House' while his wife Mamie, a Denver native, spent time with her family. From 1955 to 1958 the USAF Academy was housed at Lowry AFB while its facilities at Colorado Springs were being built. On March 13, 1958, Lowry became the first Titan I ICBM base because of its close proximity to the Titan I manufacturer, the Martin Company (now Lockheed Martin), which was located in Littleton.

Flight operations at Lowry stopped in 1966 and ten years later the US Air Force Accounting and Finance Center moved there. In 1985, a Peacekeeper ICBM maintenance shop was opened, and in 1986 a training program for space was initiated at Lowry. The base was closed in 1994, due to budget cuts.

While construction began on Red Rocks and Lowry, Colorado's farmers were recovering from the depression. These three farm images from 1939 are of Rio Grande County in the south central part of the state. **Top left** shows potato pickers loading baskets and dumping them into a horse-drawn machine that bagged them.

Top right is a tractor-drawn one-row digger that brought the potatoes to the surface, so they could be picked. And **at left** is a refrigerated truck that pre-cooled train cars before the potatoes were loaded and shipped. Arthur Rothstein took these photographs under the auspices of the FSA, which was a New Deal agency charged with photographing the life of rural Americans in the wake of the Depression.

The **top left** picture here shows farmers threshing grain on one of the homesteads of the San Luis Valley Farms near Alamosa, and the shot at **top right** is of Apolinar Rael, a rehabilitation client near Fort Garland in Costilla County, who is harvesting beans. Both are by Rothstein in 1939, as is the shot at **bottom left** showing buyers for the meat packing plants at the stockyards in Denver, all dressed up in suits and wearing white hats, too. The image at **bottom right** is a Russell Lee photograph of peach pickers' cars parked in front of a haystack in Delta County, in the west central part of the state. The town of Delta was originally a Ute trading post that existed before Fort Uncompahgre was built in 1828. Named for its situation on the delta between the Gunnison River and the Uncompahgre River, Delta was incorporated in 1882 and today is home to about 9,000 people and the famed Egyptian Movie Theatre (egyptiantheatredelta.com), built in 1928.

Below is a quintessentially Colorado picture showing the meeting of agriculture, railways and mountains. It's a Russell Lee photograph from 1940 of men in Cimarron loading fat lambs on a narrow gauge train for shipment to the Denver market.

Chapter 12
World War II

On the last day of the 1939 World Series, as the men above watched scores being posted on a chalkboard outside the Montrose newspaper, Germany was annexing the western half of Poland. Two days prior to this photograph, on October 6th, Hitler had given his Peace Plan speech in the Reichstag. In it, he maintained that the total annihilation of the Polish defenses and the country's partition between himself and Josef Stalin has removed the necessity for a German war with Britain and France. He then called for a peace conference, a restoration of Germany's colonies, and unilateral arms limitation. As he was speaking, the last 8,000 Polish troops surrendered near Warsaw.

In the World Series, the defending champion New York Yankees defeated the Cincinnati Reds for their fourth consecutive title. The Montrose Daily Press is still going strong, having served the Uncompahgre valley since 1908 with coverage of Montrose, Delta, Olathe, Ouray and Ridgway.

That Labor Day (on Monday, September 2nd), the children **at left** had lined the main street in Silverton to watch a parade. Russell Lee photographed them in their churchgoing outfits with the cars washed and waxed and everyone cheering. But Mr. Lee also snapped the sign in the shop window **below**, which bore bad news for many of their Dads.

The Shenandoah-Dives Mining Company was the largest mine employer in Silverton from the company's inception in 1927 (as an amalgamation of three mines) until the end of the Korean War in 1953, when it closed. Despite rebuilding Europe and Japan, prices for many metals dropped in those years as government munitions contracts expired. But back on Labor Day 1940, the Battle of Britain was in its 55th day, and two ships were attacked by U-boats in the North Atlantic (one sunk).

At the Labor Day celebrations, Lee also captured a group of men (**below**) cranking up an Ingersoll-Rand engine to supply what looks like compressed air for a miners' drilling contest. Note the relaxed attire of the county sheriff at the left of the picture, the eight boys sitting on the roof of a house behind the machine, and the fact that two of the men are wearing hardhats.

Some people in Denver were a little more conscious of the war. By 1940, the Hayden Ranch was one of the largest spreads still operating close to downtown Denver. That year, the government purchased the property as a site for the new Denver Ordnance Plant (DOP), and then contracted with Remington Arms Company to manufacture several million rifle and machine gun cartridges each month during the war. (Over the next few decades, the facility grew into the largest U.S. federal office venue outside Washington, DC. It houses 28 different agencies in 44 federal buildings, with a total of four million square feet of rentable space on a 623-acre campus.) In 1941, the Rocky Mountain Arsenal chemical warfare facility was begun near Denver.

In 1942, a large ordnance depot was opened about fourteen miles east of Pueblo. This was a major storage area for armaments and equipment after the war. And in 1952, chemical weapons were transferred to the Pueblo Army Depot from the Rocky Mountain Arsenal in Denver.

Lee also visited Telluride that summer of 1940, where he photographed a gradual but still startling transition that had taken place in mine operations over the preceding couple of decades. He shot an old wooden horse-drawn ore wagon that had been retired from service (**at left**: note the iron tire separating from the right front rim). And just down the road he captured a truck (**below**) with duallies hauling ore down to the smelter, carrying twice the load at three times the speed.

Given that Colorado was so rich in both mines and railroads, and the state had a central location, it doesn't seem too unbelievable that Denver would become a center for... shipbuilding! By 1942, that was actually the case. On the next page is a scene shot in May of that year by the Office of War Information, showing the interior of a ship-building plant in Denver that was "one of eight so engaged in a 56 million dollar program".

160

Parts for ships were sent from this land-locked plant in Denver to Mare Island, just north of San Francisco, for assembly. It's hard to believe that ships were built 1,300 miles from the ocean. Defense contracting ramped up at an incredible rate. In 1942 Camp Carson (renamed Fort Carson in 1954) was opened south of Colorado Springs. It was named for Kit Carson, and was designed to accommodate about 36,000 soldiers. Construction began on Camp Hale, home of the 19th Mountain, in 1942. The site was ideal for training up to 15,000 troops in skiing and mountain climbing. Located between Leadville and Vail, it was decommissioned after the war. An Army airbase was begun adjacent to the airport in Colorado Springs in 1942, and the college was used as a dorm for a while that summer.

That August, the runways were laid, and later that month a young airman, Lieutenant Ed Peterson, crashed on takeoff. Subsequently named Peterson Field, it was home to the Third Air force, Second Air Force and a fighter training school. B-29 bombers were stationed there beginning in 1943, and in 1946 the government returned control of the field to civilian authorities (the city of Colorado Springs). Today, the runways are shared between military and civilian use, and Peterson is home to several Air Force units.

The war effort involved Colorado in many ways, from food production to mining. In December of 1942, Andreas Feininger took the picture below of the American Smelting and Refining Company's smelter in Leadville. Here, lead concentrates from Creede were processed. Lead was, of course, vital to the supply of ammunition to the troops.

The company, now known as ASARCO, began life in 1899 by consolidating mine interests in Colorado, Montana, Texas and Mexico. In 1901 it merged with M. Guggenheim Sons, adding a smelter in New Jersey and several mines in Mexico. Today, having survived bankruptcy in 2009, it operates facilities all through the Americas, although its Black Cloud Mine in Leadville was shut down in 1999.

Feininger, shooting for the FSA, took the image **below** showing lead and silver mining taking place in Creede in 1942. In the early 1890s, the D&RG ran two trains a day to Crede. After the silver market collapsed in 1893, mining efforts switched primarily to lead and zinc with some silver, gold and copper.

With many able-bodied young men in uniform, the face of Colorado changed during the early 1940s. Instead of the unemployment and destitution of the Depression and the Dust Bowl, there was actually a shortage of workers. The new decade brought rain to the fields, new farming practices, a boom in mining, jobs in munitions factories, and the end of programs such as the WPA and the CCC. **Below** is an unattributed FSA photograph showing Mexican workers recruited and brought to the Arkansas Valley by the government, to harvest and process sugarbeets under contract with the Inter-mountain Agricultural Improvement Association.

Mixed with the prosperity was a general uneasiness about the progress of wars in Europe, North Africa and the Pacific. With no Internet or CNN, families with boys in uniform went through long periods where they heard no news. The only way to deal with uncertainty was to carry on at home as best one could, supporting the war effort by working hard and producing everything the armed forces needed to win. The industrialization of America during this short period was the greatest economical miracle ever seen. Often, women replaced their husbands and sons in factories and fields, playing a vital role in the national struggle.

Their courage and dedication, combined with the character of America's soldiers, sailors and airmen, caused Tom Brokaw to say this was our greatest generation. They delivered civilization from the machinations of a gang of genocidal fanatics that included Hitler, Goebbels (whom Hitler had named his successor in his will), Stalin, Hirohito and Mussolini.

While some revisionist historians would not include Hirohito in the list of fanatics, it's worth noting that he personally authorized the use of chemical weapons against the Chinese on more than 300 occasions in 1938, signed an alliance with Hitler in September 1940, personally chose and appointed the hardliner General Hideki Tōjō as Japan's prime minister over more moderate candidates, and on November 5th 1941 approved the December attacks on Pearl Harbor and the Philippines. As evidence of his fanaticism, beginning in June 1944 he ordered all Japanese civilians to commit suicide rather than be taken prisoner by American forces. (In Saipan, more than 1,000 of his subjects did so as US troops were approaching.) And his refusal to surrender when there was absolutely no hope of victory cost thousands of American lives and the destruction of two major cities, Nagasaki and Hiroshima.

Unfortunately, the actions of Hirohito and his cabinet caused a response in Colorado and across the United States that remains as one of the great blemishes on our national character. The Granada War Relocation Center, known as Camp Amache, opened 135 miles east of Pueblo (near the Kansas border) in August of 1942. The facility, shown **at left** in a War Relocation Authority image made by the government in 1942, was one of ten across the country built to imprison Japanese-Americans, and at its height it was used to incarcerate more than 7,000 detainees. The only thing that can be said is that here, people were perhaps treated better than in any of the other camps, and Amache was noted for its lack of violence and confrontation.

Here are three more images from the war years. **Top left** is a U.S. Army Signal Corps photo from c.1943 showing the 122nd Infantry Greek battalion at Camp Carson with the regimental band of the 353rd Infantry in the foreground. **Bottom left** is a U.S. Army shot of munitions workers preparing shells for fill at the Rocky Mountain Arsenal in Commerce City, also probably from 1943. And below is an FSA image from 1942 described thus: "Twenty-four hours a day the sparks from acetylene torches of steel workers in eight Denver fabricating plants are flying thick and fast [so] that the U.S. Navy may carry the battle to the enemy in all parts of the world. Here in secluded Denver, the world's largest city not on a navigable waterway, this war production worker, who has never seen a battleship or an ocean, fashions the steel hull parts which are being assembled at Mare Island Navy Yard".

Chapter 13
The Post-War Years

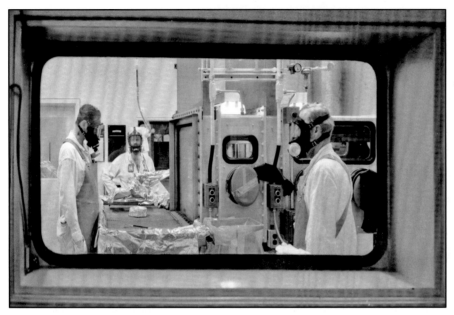

Here, we're looking through a sealed window at downdraft tables in the super dry room at Rocky Flats plutonium manufacturing facility in Golden. A government HAER photographer took this image in November 1973. Plutonium parts were assembled on these tables.

Between 1950 and 2010, the state's population rose from about 1.3 million to just over five million, most of the increase being in the Front Range and the Denver metropolitan area.

Defense Industry

Churchill had warned America that "an iron curtain" would descend across Eastern Europe after WWII, signaling the beginning of a new struggle, the Cold War. The detonation of two nuclear devices over Japan in 1945 ushered in the Atomic Age, and with it the threat of mutual destruction. In Colorado, the federal government's first major move in this new chess game was to begin construction of the Rocky Flats plant in 1951. This was a nuclear weapons production facility near Denver, Colorado that operated from 1952 until 1977 under the auspices of the Atomic Energy Commission, and thereafter until 1992 as an arm of the Department of Energy. In 1957, a fire at the plant released radioactive plutonium into Denver airspace.

A second plutonium fire in 1969 was more extensive. The AEC was slow to disclose any evidence of contamination, which in some cases was quite severe in the Denver area. The limited disclosure and subsequent reports caused a public outcry. In 1989, a joint EPA and FBI raid stopped weapons production at the facility. In 1954 and '55, the United States built and then opened a new Air Force Academy just north of Colorado Springs. There were 306 cadets in the class of 1959, which was sworn in on a hot afternoon in July 1955 at Lowry AFB in Denver. A strategic and historic agreement was realized in 1958 when the US and Canada formed NORAD at Ent AFB in Colorado Springs. Three years later, contractors began drilling tunnels to locate the facility underground and in 1966 the Cheyenne Mountain Combat Ops center was operational. However, in 2006, NORAD was moved from there to Peterson AFB.

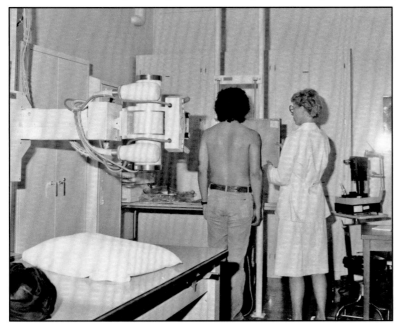

In this HAER government photo taken in Building 122, an employee or a subcontractor working at Rocky Flats undergoes a routine medical check-up that includes X-ray exams. (October 1985)

In 1962, in an event that rings warning bells in the minds of people affected by modern oil fracking, there were several small earthquakes around the Rocky Mountain Arsenal when administrators tried to dispose of hazardous waste in a deep shaft. That year, the first Atlas Missile sites in Colorado were prepared under the auspices of Warren AFB in Cheyenne, Wyoming. A second underground event called Project Rulison involved the detonation of a nuclear device in the vicinity of the town of Grand Valley (now Parachute) in the far west of the state. Detonated in the fall of 1969, it was designed to release natural gas deposits for harvest. It succeeded, but the gas was so radioactive it could not be used for domestic purposes.

Four years later, the government detonated three more nuclear devices in Colorado, this time near Rifle, in Rio Blanco County. The 33 kTN (kiloton) bombs were located at three levels in a sandstone well, approximately 1/3 to ½ mile underground. Again, the goal was the harvest of natural gas. Results can't have been too encouraging as the effort to use nuclear explosives for a peaceful purpose essentially terminated with this test.

Space and the Mile High State

Colorado has had strong connections with the Space Program almost from its inception. In 1962 a Boulder native, Scott Carpenter, was the second American to orbit the earth (the first was John Glenn). He had been one of the original seven test pilots selected for NASA's Mercury project back in April 1959. He earned a Bachelor of Science degree in aeronautical engineering from the University of Colorado in 1949. Carpenter spent thirty days during the summer of 1965 living and working in a sea-floor habitat, 205 feet below the surface. The term used to describe a person who does this is 'aquanaut', and

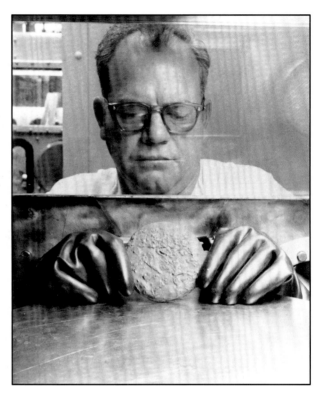

In this 1973 HAER photograph, a worker at the Rocky Mountain Flats plant holds a plutonium 'button', an amalgam of scraps of the rare material

Carpenter became one in the Sealab II program, which was located off the coast of La Jolla, California. In retirement, he lived in Vail and loved to ski. Scott Carpenter passed away on October 10th 2013.

Jack Swigert, a Denver kid, was among the crew of Apollo 13 when they survived a harrowing mission that included an oxygen tank explosion, loss of most of the electrical power, cabin heat and potable water, and a dysfunctional CO2 treatment device. Actor Kevin Bacon played Swigert in the 1995 Ron Howard/Tom Hanks movie about the voyage.

In 1995, a private company called EchoStar Communications, located in Englewood, successfully launched a satellite. The business provides "advanced satellite communications solutions including video distribution, data communications and backhaul services for media and broadcast, enterprise, government and military customers". By 2014, the company had 23 satellites in orbit.

These two HAER images from 1989 show (above) a westward view over the launch doors of a Titan One missile silo near Aurora, and at right, inside the decommissioned bay.

Advances in Transportation

On January 19th 1952 a new turnpike opened between Denver and Boulder. The concept for the road is attributed to Professor Rod Downing of the School of Engineering at Colorado University, and the original goal was to build a toll road. However, feasibility studies said that funds collected on the road wouldn't suffice, so a bond issue was formed, too. The original toll was 25¢.

In 1958, construction began in the northeastern corner of the state on what would eventually become I-76. And in 1962 engineers began looking for a way to run an Interstate under, rather than across, the Continental Divide. To that end, crews began drilling the Eisenhower-Johnson Memorial Tunnel for I-70 near the Loveland Pass in 1969. It was completed ten years later, is about 1-2/3 miles long, and is the highest vehicular tunnel in the US at an elevation of just over 11,000 feet.

I-25 was completed in 1969, and in 1970 the last leg of I-270 opened. The last piece of Colorado's Interstate system was opened to the public in 1993 with the dedication of the interchange between I-76 and I-25.

In 1971 the US Dept. of Transportation's Federal Railroad Administration (FRA) opened the Transportation Technology Center (TTC) in Pueblo. Initially called the High Speed Ground Test Center, its longest stretch (13-1/2 miles) of track is used for high-speed testing up to 165 mph, while other tracks test third rail electric trains, and cars and diesels under extreme conditions. The center also houses labs, a crash wall and various other testing facilities designed to improve rail safety.

The Regional Transportation District (RTD) was organized in 1969. It administers public transportation systems in an eight-county Denver/Boulder metro area. In 1994, RTD (online at rtd-denver.com) began light rail service in Denver.

A HABS image from 1955 shows a home at Hudson Road and 96th Avenue, at the east edge of what is now the International Airport (DIA).

The following year, Denver International Airport opened, replacing the old Stapleton International Airport (see photo **at left**).

In 2006 the ambitious Transportation Expansion Project (T-REX) was completed, expanding the width of many Interstate approaches by adding lanes, and constructing 19 miles of new light rail in the metro area. It came in under budget and ahead of schedule. In 2014, RTD reopened Union Station in Denver after a massive renovation project spearheaded by the construction firm of Milender White. Combining trains, light rail, bus service, retail space and a 112-room hotel, the historic Union Station "has been revitalized as the centerpiece of a bustling downtown".

Arts and Industry

The first commercial television broadcaster in Colorado hit the airwaves on July 18th 1952. At the time there were eight radio stations and two major newspapers in the Denver area. KFEL-TV (Channel 2) was the first new station in America following the Korean War. The first announcers at KFEL were Bob Shriver and Merwin Smith.

In 1955, Colorado had its first Miss America. As a freshman at Colorado Women's College, Sharon Ritchie won the Miss Colorado pageant at age 18. During a successful career in television and theatre, she and her husband Don Cherry had two sons, Sean and Stephan. Tragically, her younger son Stephen died in the attack on the north tower of the World Trade Center. Marilyn Van Derbur of Denver won the title in 1958, and Rebecca Ann King, a graduate of the University of Denver School of Law, won in 1974.

According to the MillerCoors website (millercoors.com), "Adolph Coors apprenticed at a brewery in Prussia during his teens and stowed away on a ship to America to realize his dreams of becoming a brewer. Adolph opened the Golden Brewery (later Coors Brewing Company) in Colorado and tapped his first barrel in 1873". The first aluminum beer can was launched at the Coors Golden Brewery on January 22nd 1959, and today Coors operates one of the largest aluminum can producing plants in the world (Rocky Mountain Metal Container in Golden). In February of the following year, Adolph Coors III was murdered. His assailant, Joseph Corbett Jr. (aka Walter Osborne) was attempting to kidnap him near the Coors family home in Bear Creek Canyon, west of Denver. Today, the Coors brewery in Golden is the largest single-site brewery facility in the world. During Prohibition, the company produced malted milk for the Mars Candy factories, and a product called Manna, which was non-alcoholic beer. They also operated a porcelain manufacturing plant (now called CoorsTek). Over the years the company had some run-ins with unions. It was accused of discrimination against gays and lesbians in the 1970s, but in recent years has been one of a handful of major employers to extend employee benefits to same-sex partners.

Adolph Coors (1847-1929)

Coors has been a vital part of Golden's economy and Colorado's popular culture for almost a hundred and fifty years. One obvious example is the naming rights at Coors Field, home of the Colorado Rockies baseball team.

The Tivoli Brewery (**above**, in a William Barrett HABS photo from 1980) was constructed in 1890 at a site located from 1320 to 1348 Tenth St. It came into being even before Adolph Coors tapped his first barrel: its story began with a wagon trip in 1859, when James Good brought a load of hops to Charles Endlich's new facility in Denver, the Rocky Mountain Brewing Co. Good had been a brewer in Europe (probably Denmark). He eventually bought/inherited the Denver operation, and renamed it Tivoli in 1870, apparently after the gardens in Copenhagen. Around the turn of the century the company consolidated with the Union Brewery and the Milwaukee Brewery under the name Tivoli-Union. It ceased operation in 1969. In the 1980s it was a shopping mall and then vacant, and since 1994 it has been the Tivoli Student Union, which houses the Auraria Campus Bookstore, restaurants, a credit union, meeting spaces and retail outlets. The image at left is a large copper kettle on the second floor, also a HABS image by Barrett in 1980.

Another Colorado institution, John Denver, was actually born in Roswell, New Mexico in 1943. (He was 3-1/2 years old when the aliens landed there, so he probably wasn't involved.) His birth name was Henry John Deutschendorf. In the mid-sixties his first real musician's job was with the Chad Mitchell Trio, an all-man group who still sing folk songs (chadmitchelltrio.com). Another folk group, Peter, Paul and Mary, recorded one of Deutschendorf's songs on an album (called *Album 1700*) in 1967, and released it as a single in 1969. *Leaving On A Jet Plane* was a hit. The songwriter changed his name to John Denver, signed with Mercury RCA, released his first single (*Rhymes and Reasons)*, and a legend was born. Denver was immensely proud of the Rockies and the city whose name he took, and his song *Rocky Mountain High* has become an anthem for the state of Colorado. It was adopted as the second State Song with the passage of SJR07-023 on March 12, 2007. (A.J. Flynn's *Where The Columbines Grow* was adopted as the first state song on May 8, 1915, by an act of the General Assembly). John Denver died in a plane crash on October 12th 1997. He was the pilot.

The Telluride Film Festival (telluridefilmfestival.org) began in 1973 and takes place every Labor Day Weekend. Some of the movies that have debuted at the festival include *Blue Velvet*, *Crouching Tiger Hidden Dragon*, *Brokeback Mountain*, *The Last King of Scotland*, *Juno* and *The King's Speech*. Visitors in the past have run into celebrities such as Meryl Streep, Penelope Cruz and Bill Murray on the streets of Telluride during the Festival. But, as with many locations in Colorado, the real star of the show is the breathtaking scenery all around.

From January 1981 until May 1989, Colorado entered living rooms all across America each week as the location of the television show Dynasty. It was the saga of a wealthy Denver family in the oil business and starred John Forsythe, Linda Evans and Joan Collins. Heather Locklear, Diahann Carroll, Rock Hudson, Billy Dee Williams, Emma Samms, Ken Howard, Ricardo Montalban and a host of other noted actors played roles. Other series set in Colorado were *Dr. Quinn, Medicine Woman*, and *Mork & Mindy*, starring the late Robin Williams. Tim Allen was born in Denver, too.

In 1982, downtown Denver's personality changed with the construction of the 16th Street Mall. A pedestrian area lined with trees, it features outdoor cafes, restaurants, shopping, and a number of historically preserved buildings interspersed within a contemporary urban environment. Visionary design elements include height restrictions to allow sunlight on the street, public art and free shuttle buses that travel the length of the mile-long Mall every day of the week.

The Colorado Convention Center opened in downtown Denver in 1990. It is "located within easy walking distance of over 8,700 hotel rooms, 300 restaurants, 9 theatres of the Denver Performing Arts Complex and a wide variety of shopping and retail outlets". It is the largest LEED certified building (environmentally conscious) in Colorado, and even includes an on-site farm that produces 3,600 pounds of fruits, vegetables and herbs annually, for use by in-house chefs.

Science in the Spotlight

Colorado has an impressive record in academia, research and learning on the world stage. In 1958, Boulder native Edward Lawrie Tatum shared a Nobel Prize with George Wells Beadle for illustrating the relationship between genes and biochemical processes, thus helping to create the field of study in molecular genetics. In 1987, Professor Thomas Robert Cech of the University of Colorado Boulder shared the 1989 Nobel Prize in for the discovery of catalytic properties of RNA. In 2001, University of Colorado Boulder researcher Professor Eric Cornell shared the Nobel Prize in Physics for revealing Bose-Einstein condensation. In 2005, researcher John Hall of the University of Colorado Boulder shared the Nobel Prize in Physics for contributions to the development of laser-based precision spectroscopy. And in 2012, David Wineland, a physicist at the U.S. Department of Commerce's National Institute of Standards and Technology lab in Boulder shared the Nobel Prize in Physics for what the Royal Swedish Academy of Sciences said was "ground-breaking experimental methods that enable measuring and manipulation of individual quantum systems".

Alfred Nobel was a Swedish chemist and the inventor of dynamite. The first Nobel Prize was awarded in 1901.

Surgeon Thomas Earl Starzl served on the faculty of the University of Colorado in Denver from 1962 to 1980. He was also the Director of Surgery at the Denver Veterans' Administration Hospital from 1962 to 1972. He was a pioneer in organ transplant research and immunology, and among the first to successfully complete the procedure, using a combination of cyclosporine and prednisone. According to the University of Pittsburgh: "eleven of the first 12 liver recipients treated in Colorado with cyclosporine-based immunosuppression during 1979-80 survived for more than one year".

In 1974, the Solar Energy Research Institute was created, and it began operations in 1977 on a campus in Golden. Today, it is the National Renewable Energy Laboratory (nrel.gov), with a mission to provide sustainable alternatives for powering our homes, businesses and transportation system.

As of late 2014, the United Nations Educational, Scientific and Cultural Organization (UNESCO) had listed 1,007 sites around the world that are the subjects of international agreements to secure the planet's cultural and natural heritage. In 1978, Mesa Verde National Park was named a World Heritage Site.

In 1987, the National Mining Hall of Fame and Museum moved into its present 71,000 square foot building that has been the Leadville Junior High School and, before that, Leadville High School. The building was constructed in 1899, and the Museum is an extensive five-level complex that has been called the Smithsonian of the Rockies.

The Sand Creek Massacre National Historic Site was dedicated as the 391st unit of the nation's National Park system on April 28th 2007. In 2010 some water line workers discovered the skeleton of a young female mastodon near Snowmass Village and the site eventually yielded more than 4,000 bones from 26 Ice Age vertebrates.

In 2012, History Colorado opened the History Colorado Center, "a vibrant place where people experience the past from entirely new perspectives. Located at 12th and Broadway in Denver's Golden Triangle Museum District, this award-winning building was designed and constructed by an all-Colorado team." History Colorado was established in 1879 and is a 501(c)(3) charitable organization. It's an agency of the State of Colorado, under the Department of Higher Education. To become a member or to learn more about the new museum, visit historycolorado.org or call (303) 447-8679.

Natural Disasters

The South Platte flows essentially from south of Vail to the west side of Pike's Peak, and then runs northwest past Denver to the corner of the state where it enters Nebraska. In 1965, there was a major flood that cost 28 lives and half a billion dollars in damage from Littleton through Fort Morgan, Brush and Sterling.

In the wake of a ten to twelve inch of rainfall in four hours on the afternoon of July 31st 1976, a flood in Big Thompson Canyon west of Loveland cost 143 lives. (It was originally thought the number was 144, but a survivor was discovered in Oklahoma in 2009.)

A wildfire on Storm King Mountain near Glenwood Springs in 1994 claimed the lives of 14 firefighters, in what became known as the South Canyon Fire.

In 2002, Colorado's largest wildfire ever was probably started deliberately. Terry Lynn Barton, a US Forest Service worker, was convicted of so doing. The Hayman fire was located 95 miles southwest of Denver and 35 miles northwest of Colorado Springs. It burned 138,000 acres, destroyed 133 homes, and forced the evacuation of 8,000 people. Tragically, five firefighters died on their way to fight the blaze. Most of the damage occurred in the Pike National Forest. Barton was sentenced to six years in federal prison and was ordered to reimburse the government in the amount of $14.6m. She was released in 2008.

That same month (June, 2002), another wildfire in the mountains north of Durango claimed a firefighter's life (Alan Wayne Wyatt, 51, from Ontario, Oregon). The Missionary Ridge fire burned for 39 days, destroyed 56 homes and razed 73,000 acres. In September 2010 a fire started in Four Mile Canyon just west of Boulder that would eventually destroy 169 homes and burn about 6,000 acres.

2012 was a tough year in Colorado. A prairie grass fire near Last Chance swept across 40,000 acres and took four homes and a number of other buildings. The town (population 23) is halfway between Fort Morgan and Limon, 80 miles straight east of Denver. On June 9, lightning started the High Park fire west of Fort Collins, and it burned for 21 days, killing one woman. The fire consumed almost 90,000 acres and more than 250 homes. In the

Prairie storm, photo by author 2014.

middle of it, on June 23rd, a new fire began west of Colorado Springs. That conflagration, known as the Waldo Canyon fire, would eventually destroy 18,000 acres, evacuate some 32,000 residents from Colorado Springs, and consume about 350 homes.

In June the following year, a complex of three fires erupted near Wolf Creek Pass (**see photo on next page**). The first was in the West Fork area near Pagosa Springs. Then the Papoose fire started near Creede, and a third but smaller blaze began near the Wolf Creek Ski resort. Just to the north, the Wild Rose Fire burned more than 1,000 acres and threatened many natural gas wells that Encana Oil and Gas reportedly shut down. The next week, a lightning fire in the Big Meadows of Rocky Mountain National Park burned about 600 acres. The same day, a major fire started north of Colorado Springs in the Black Forest that would take some 500 homes (to date the most in Colorado history).

The Black Forest fire also burned more than 14,000 acres and 38,000 people had to be evacuated. Within hours, a third fire began at Royal Gorge near Canon City, burning an aerial tram car and buildings on either side of the gorge, and doing some minor damage to the famous bridge.

Climate change became very real to Coloradoans in September 2013 when floods along the entire Front Range took nine lives, completely destroyed some 1,800 homes and caused an estimated three billion dollars worth of damage.

In the photograph **above**, which was taken by astronauts aboard the International Space Station on June 19th 2013, smoke from the West Fork Complex fire (1) can clearly be seen in the foreground. Just to the left of center in the picture, one can make out the plume of the Wild Rose fire (2), and immediately below the West Fork is a small plume from the Wolf Creek blaze (3).

Political Milestones

In November 1972, a thirty-two year old Denver Democrat named Patricia Schroeder was the first female elected to Congress by the state of Colorado. Armed with a degree from Harvard Law School, the Portland, Oregon native moved to Colorado in 1964 to take a job with the National Labor Relations Board. She then worked for Planned Parenthood, and also taught in public schools.

She would go on to serve 24 years in Congress, being re-elected eleven times. Schroeder was the first woman to serve on the House Armed Services Committee and she ran for President in 1988.

Pat Schroeder represented Colorado's First Congressional District for 24 years. (Congressional Pictorial Directory, 97th Congress, c.1982)

The year Schroeder took her seat (1973), Denver became the first public school district in a northern state to be ordered by the Supreme Court to desegregate its student body (the Keyes decision).

In 1984 and again in 1988, Senator Gary Hart (born Hartpence) ran for the Presidency. Today, he is the US Special Envoy to Northern Ireland, appointed by President Obama in 2014. Hart, a native of Kansas, was George McGovern's campaign manager in 1972. He also served on the Armed Services Committee, and was a member of the Church Committee that investigated the assassination of John Kennedy. In the 1984 campaign, Walter Mondale's "Where's the beef?" remark undercut Hart's rising star, and

Senator Gary Hart of Colorado. (U.S. Senate Historical Office.)

ultimately Mondale became the nominee. In the '88 election, Schroeder was his campaign chairperson. Hart was the object of a scandal that involved model Donna Rice, after which he dropped out of the race and Schroeder briefly entered in his place. Hart has been on the fringes of politics ever since. In 2002 he briefly considered running again for the Presidency, but quickly changed his mind.

In 1992, Colorado's voters approved TABOR decrees states that state and local governments can't raise tax rates without voter approval, or can't spend revenues collected under existing tax rates if revenues grow faster than the rate of inflation and population growth, without voter approval.

In 2006, Colorado voters approved Amendment 43, which banned same-sex marriage. The ballot question read: "An amendment to the Colorado constitution, concerning marriage, and, in connection therewith, specifying that only a union of one man and one woman shall be valid or recognized as a marriage in Colorado". On March 21st 2013, Governor John Hickenlooper signed the Civil Unions Act into law at the Colorado History Museum in Denver. The Colorado General Assembly passed SB-11, which went into effect on May 1, 2013, essentially grants same-sex couples similar rights to married couples without recognizing same-sex marriage.

Above: Presidential candidate Barack Obama, his wife Michelle, and their children Malia and Sasha wave to the audience at the 2008 Democratic National Convention in Denver. (Photo courtesy of the Carol M. Highsmith Archive at the Library of Congress, also with Ms. Highsmith's personal permission.)

In August of 2008, Colorado hosted the Democratic National Convention at the Pepsi Center (the Can, home to the Denver Nuggets basketball, Colorado Avalanche hockey and Colorado Mammoth lacrosse teams) in downtown Denver. The convention delegates nominated Barack Obama, a senator from Illinois, as the party's candidate that November, and Senator Joe Biden of Delaware as Vice President. Obama accepted the nomination on August 28 at Invesco Field (Sports Authority Field at Mile High) before a crowd of 84,000 supporters, and subsequently was elected President.

Golda Meir, the first woman Prime Minister of Israel, lived in Denver. She was born Golda Mabovitch in Kiev in the Ukraine, in 1898. Her family moved to Milwaukee in 1906, refugees from Russian pogroms. She lived at 1606 Julian Street in Denver (the house is shown **above** in a HABS photograph from 1980) with her sister Sheyna, for about a year in 1912-13. She, her sister and her sister's husband emigrated to Palestine, then a British Mandate surrounded by the Ottoman Empire, in 1921. She served as Prime Minister from 1969 until 1974. The Denver house was relocated to the Auraria Campus of the Metropolitan State University of Denver in September 1988 and is now home to the Golda Meir Center for Political Leadership and the Golda Meir Museum.

Law and Order Milestones

In February of 1960, Adolph Coors III, the heir to the Coors brewing fortune, was murdered on his way to work. He was 44 years old.

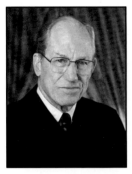

In 1962, Fort Collins native Byron White was the first Coloradoan appointed to the US Supreme Court, where he served until 1993. Justice White (**at left**, in an official portrait) had attended the University of Colorado on a scholarship, where he graduated first in his class. He was a Rhodes scholar at Oxford, and graduated from Yale Law School. Before Yale, he played pro football with both the Pittsburg Steelers (they were the Pirates back then) and the Detroit Lions, and led the league in rushing in both 1938 and 1940. He then served in the Navy in World War II, where he was awarded two Bronze Stars. White later practiced law in Denver, where he managed John Kennedy's 1960 Colorado campaign. In 1961, he was appointed United States Deputy Attorney General. Justice White passed away in 2002.

On June 18th 1984, Denver talk show host and radio commentator Alan Berg was gunned down outside his home. Members of a neo-Nazi gang called The Order carried out the attack.

In 1996, a deeply tragic incident sparked a media circus in Boulder: six-year-old JonBenét Ramsey was found murdered in the basement of her home. The case remains open.

In 1999 a massacre at Columbine High School resulted in the murders of twelve students and a teacher, the wounding of twenty-four other victims, and the suicides of the two perpetrators, who were seniors at the school.

In October of 2009, Colorado was once more in national headlines when a homemade balloon was filmed flying across the northeastern corner of the state, and a man claimed his 6-year-old son was aboard. It was revealed as an attempt to gain publicity by the family (who may have been planning a reality television show) that became known as the Balloon Boy Hoax.

In 2012, the state suffered through another heartbreaking incident when a gunman opened fire in an Aurora cinema, murdering twelve people and wounding sixty more. The alleged perpetrator was arrested and has not been tried as of October 2014, principally because the courts are awaiting psychiatric evaluations.

Also in 2012, Colorado voters approved Amendment 64 to the state's Constitution, which essentially allowed communities to regulate marijuana much in the same way that alcohol was treated. The first retail distribution stores opened on January 1st 2014.

Chapter 14
Sports and Recreation

Winter Park in 1950
Courtesy Steve Hurlbert/Grand County Historical Society/Winter Park Resort.

No history of Colorado would be complete without winter sports. There are dozens of major venues and hundreds of minor ones all across the central and western portions of the state where downhill and cross-country skiing, snowboarding, snowmobiling, ice fishing, snow shoeing, ice skating and other outdoor pursuits take advantage of the slopes and weather. Here's a list of the main downhill and boarding resorts along with the years they opened and the closest towns:

Courtesy Anthony Tallo, Eldora Mountain Resort

Howelsen Hill	1914	Steamboat Springs
Loveland	1936	Loveland
Monarch Mountain	1936	Salida
Wolf Creek	1938	Pagosa Springs
Winter Park	1939	Winter Park
Ski Cooper	1941	Leadville
Arapahoe Basin	1946	Dillon
Aspen Mountain (Ajax)	1946	Aspen
Beaver Creek	1956	Avon
Aspen Highlands	1958	Aspen
Buttermilk	1958	Aspen
Crested Butte	1960	Gunnison
Breckenridge	1961	Breckenridge
Kendall Mountain	1961	Silverton
Eldora	1962	Nederland
Hesperus Ski Area	1962	Hesperus
Vail	1962	Vail
Steamboat	1963	Steamboat
Durango Mtn/Purgatory	1965	Durango
Powderhorn	1966	Grand Junction
Sunlight	1966	Glenwood Springs
Snowmass	1967	Snowmass
Keystone	1970	Keystone
Copper Mountain	1971	Copper Mountain
Telluride	1972	Telluride
Granby Ranch	1985	Granby
Silverton Mountain	2002	Silverton

Downhill skiing was popular before World War II, but it was expensive to travel and the state was still dealing with the depression and the Dust Bowl. There weren't too many good roads through the mountains, and the cars weren't always reliable. But many of Colorado's early settlers had Scandinavian and German roots, and many others came from alpine areas in France, Italy, Austria and even Switzerland. Snow was no stranger.

*The official photograph **above** was taken in September 1908 and shows the US Olympic team that would compete in London the next month, with President Roosevelt in the white shirt, center. The team wasn't very representative of the nation. There are only two non-Caucasians and no women. Of the 2,008 athletes from twenty-two nations, only 37 were women (the first year they were allowed to participate). The only winter sport was ice-skating at the Prince's Club in Knightsbridge. Only one American male, Irving Brokaw of New York, competed and came in sixth. The first Winter Games would not be held for another sixteen years (1924) in Chamonix, France.*

During World War II, troops trained in the Rockies for mountain and winter combat. After the war, movies such as 1954's *White Christmas*, which takes place at the Pine Tree Ski Lodge in Vermont, helped spread the understanding that winter sports were becoming easier to access: the roads were better, the economy was booming, airlines were affordable and for the first time since the Twenties, people weren't hungry, or at war.

Although the resort on Aspen Mountain was only four years old, and it had only one lift when it opened, the Federation Internationale De Ski (FIS) chose to hold the 1950 Alpine World Ski Championships at Ajax Mountain. It was the first time the event had ever been held outside Europe. And just to ice the cake, the Nordic World Championship was also held in the US that year, although warm weather at Lake Placid caused the venue to be moved to Rumford (in Maine).

By 1968, when Peggy Fleming won gold in Grenoble, most American homes had television and the Winter Games became a household event. The next year, the International Olympic Committee (IOC) selected Denver as the venue for the 1976 Winter Games (until 1992, the summer and winter games were held in the same year). However, Colorado voters looked at the amount of money Montreal was spending on the summer events – the city ended up losing almost a billion dollars – and in November of 1972 Colorado's electorate rejected a bond issue to fund the XII Olympics. Denver was forced to withdraw its bid, and became the only host city ever to decline an awarded Olympic Games. The IOC turned to Innsbruck, Austria, a city with a lot of experience organizing the event (they had hosted in 1964), and it was very successful.

On January 27th 2014 the Denver Post reported that: "the final U.S. Olympic Team of 230 athletes – the largest U.S. team in Winter Games history – includes 19 Colorado athletes; 14 men

Making snow. Courtesy Anthony Tallo/Eldora Mountain Resort

and five women. Only California is fielding more Olympians, at 20, half of whom are women."

In Sochi, Jeremy Abbot from Aspen took the bronze in team, Alex Deibold from Boulder won bronze in snowboarding, Gus Kenworthy of Telluride won silver in ski slopestyle and Mikaela Shiffrin of Vail took gold in slalom skiing. Todd Lodwick of Steamboat Springs carried the flag in the opening ceremony.

Some of the older ski resorts in Colorado are well known around the world. Winter Park Resort is the state's longest continually operated ski resort. It's located about 67 miles northwest of Denver and is an amalgamation of several small villages. One of them was Hideaway Park, a cabin resort that Doc Graves started putting together back in 1932. The town of Winter Park wasn't incorporated until 1979. It is or was the home of several Olympic, US and World Champion skiers, including Michelle Roark and Elizabeth McIntyre. Today, the City and County of Denver own the resort. The town of Winter Park annexed the facility in 2006 and, because the top of the runs are at 12,060 feet, the town can now claim it has the highest elevation of any incorporated municipality in America. However, the downtown area itself is actually about 1,500 feet lower than Alma, Colorado (10,578).

Enjoying the powder on Sunlight Mountain in the 1980s.
Courtesy Jennie Spillane/Sunlight Mountain Resort

The Sunlight Ranch Company (**at right**) opened for business on December 16, 1966 on 420 acres of private land and 2081 acres of U.S. Forest Service (U.S.F.S.) land, under a 30-year U.S.F.S. special use permit. In 1966, with a handful of trails and one chairlift, Sunlight catered to 15,000 skier days. By the late 1990s, that number passed 100,000. What skiers have always found enticing about Sunlight is that it's affordable, and not too crowded so the powder lasts for days.

Aspen, like so many Colorado winter sports destinations, hosts several resorts. Located 158 miles southwest of Denver, it actually encompasses four ski areas: Aspen Mountain, Highlands, Buttermilk and Snowmass. The area is rich in downhill history, beginning with the first efforts to change the fortunes of the old silver town when Walter Paepcke saw its potential grow right after the war. The son of a Prussian immigrant, Paepcke was an executive with the Container Corp. of America, which was based in Chicago. He visited Aspen with his wife, Elizabeth in 1945, and his first chair lift opened in 1946.

Other Sports

Colorado has also been well represented over the years in the Summer Games. In 1972, for example, Frank Shorter of Boulder won the marathon in Munich. He went on to co-found the 10K Bolder Boulder in 1979. In 1996/2000, Amy Van Dyken of Englewood won six Olympic gold medals in swimming. And in 2012, Missy Franklin of Centennial won four gold medals in swimming at the Olympics in London.

Professional sports have always had a strong presence here, too. In 1978, 1987, 1988 and 1990 the Denver Broncos™ won the AFC™ Championships. Unfortunately, they weren't as lucky at the Super Bowl™ those years, but they took it all in 1998 and again in 1999 under the able leadership of quarterback John Elway. They were AFC champions again in 2014 but lost to Seattle in the Super Bowl.

The University of Colorado Buffaloes™ football team has been playing since 1890 and exactly 100 years later they won the Orange Bowl™ and the Associated Press national championship. Then, in 1994, the Buffaloes' Rashaan Salaam took home the 1994 Heisman Trophy™.

The Colorado Avalanche™ won the Stanley Cup™ in 1996, and again in 2001.

In 2007, the Colorado Rockies™ won the National League™ Pennant.

And in 2010, the Colorado Rapids™ won the Major League Soccer Cup championship.

~

A Brief Cameo:
George H. Welch of Craig took the following two photos in 1920. Actually, they were all on one panoramic image, and we have separated them just so they fit on the page. The top one (the right half of the photograph) shows the Meeker High School girls' basketball team and the boys' football team.

The lower image is the Craig High School boys' football team and girls' basketball team. Meeker and Craig are located in the northwest corner of the state. Of the photographer, we know that he was still taking photographs in 1950, that in 1908 he and his wife lost their six-month-old daughter, Margaret after a brief, two-day illness, and that both he and his wife Julia lived from 1881 to 1969, and they are buried in the Fairview Cemetery.

Colorado's Governors

Gov. John Hickenlooper	(2011 -)	Democrat
Gov. Bill Ritter	(2007 - 2011)	Democrat
Gov. Bill Owens	(1999 - 2007)	Republican
Gov. Roy Romer	(1987 - 1999)	Democrat
Gov. Richard D. Lamm	(1975 - 1987)	Democrat
Gov. John D. Vanderhoof	(1973 - 1975)	Republican
Gov. John Arthur Love	(1963 - 1973)	Republican
Gov. Stephen Lucid Robert McNichols	(1957 - 1963)	Democrat
Gov. Daniel Issac J. Thornton	(1951 - 1955)	Republican
Gov. Walter Walfred Johnson	(1950 - 1951)	Democrat
Gov. William Lee Knous	(1947 - 1950)	Democrat
Gov. John Charles Vivian	(1943 - 1947)	Republican
Gov. Ralph Lawrence Carr	(1939 - 1943)	Republican
Gov. Teller Ammons	(1937 - 1939)	Democrat
Gov. Raymond Herbert Talbot	(1937 - 1937)	Democrat
Gov. Edwin Carl Johnson	(1933 - 1937)	Democrat
And...	(1955 - 1957)	Democrat
Gov. William Herbert Adams	(1927 - 1933)	Democrat
Gov. Clarence Morley	(1925 - 1927)	Republican
Gov. William Ellery Sweet	(1923 - 1925)	Democrat
Gov. Oliver Henry Nelson Shoup	(1919 - 1923)	Republican
Gov. Julius Caldeen Gunter	(1917 - 1919)	Democrat
Gov. George Alfred Carlson	(1915 - 1917)	Republican
Gov. Elias Milton Ammons	(1913 - 1915)	Democrat
Gov. John Franklin Shafroth	(1909 - 1913)	Republican, Democrat
Gov. Henry Augustus Buchtel	(1907 - 1909)	Republican
Gov. Jesse Fuller McDonald	(1905 - 1907)	Republican
Gov. James Hamilton Peabody	(1903 - 1905)	Republican
And...	(1905 - 1905)	Republican
Gov. James Bradley Orman	(1901 - 1903)	Democrat
Gov. Charles Spalding Thomas	(1899 - 1901)	Democrat
Gov. Albert Wills McIntire	(1895 - 1897)	Republican
Gov. Davis Hanson Waite	(1893 - 1895)	Populist
Gov. Job Adams Cooper	(1889 - 1891)	Republican
Gov. Alva Adams	(1887 - 1889)	Democrat
And...	(1897 - 1899)	Democrat
And...	(1905 - 1905)	Democrat
Gov. Benjamin Harrison Eaton	(1885 - 1887)	Republican
Gov. James Benton Grant	(1883 - 1885)	Democrat
Gov. Frederick Walker Pitkin	(1879 - 1883)	Republican
Gov. John Long Routt	(1875 - 1879)	Republican
And...	(1891 - 1893)	Republican

INDEX

In August 1947 Robert W. Richardson photographed the 346 (above) in Dolores. The narrow gauge locomotive was purchased in 1946 from the D&RG and hauled lumber to the sawmill for two years until a fire destroyed the mill and the line was scrapped.

Parting thoughts...

In 1944, three years before the photograph above was made, travelogue director James A. FitzPatrick narrated an 8-minute short titled *Colorful Colorado* that was played in movie theatres across the country. Some of the things he mentioned were that 43% of Colorado was publicly owned land, and that there were 6,000 miles of streams and 2,000 trout lakes within the state's borders.

Seventy years later, the fishing is still great. In 2011 (the latest year for which stats are available), some 57,900,000 people visited Colorado! And of all the folks who spent time at ski resorts in America from Vermont to California, a whopping 18.6% chose to do so in Colorado. The state was also ninth in outdoor recreation such as backpacking, hiking and camping. It is home to the world's largest elk population (nearly a quarter of a million head), and more than 80 species of fish.

With abundant sunshine and some of the cleanest air and water on the planet, visitors can walk in the footsteps of dinosaurs and desperados, miners and mountain men, and enjoy views that are unparalleled anywhere else. Within the borders of this unbelievable place one can find quiet solitude or adrenaline-pumping excitement in the mountains, a sense of spirituality and place on the Great Plains, and the art and culture of one of the world's greatest cities.

It's the kind of place where history lives.

To order copies of this book, visit

TheColoradoBook.com